MENTAL HEALTH

AND THE

CHURCH

A Ministry Handbook for Including Children
and Adults with ADHD, Anxiety, Mood Disorders,
and Other Common Mental Health Conditions

Stephen Grcevich, MD

ZONDERVAN®

ZONDERVAN

Mental Health and the Church
Copyright © 2018 by Stephen Grcevich

This title is also available as a Zondervan ebook.

Requests for information should be addressed to:
Zondervan, 3900 Sparks Dr. SE, Grand Rapids, Michigan 49546

ISBN 978-0-310-53481-5

Published in association with the literary agency of Credo Communications, LLC,
Grand Rapids, Michigan, www.credocommunications.net.

Cover design: RAMCreative
Cover photos: iStockphoto, Pexels
Interior design: Kait Lamphere

Printed in the United States of America

17 18 19 20 21 22 23 24 25 26 /DHV/ 15 14 13 12 11 10 9 8 7 6 5 4 3 2 1

In this thoughtful, compassionate, and practical book, Stephen Grcevich provides a great resource destined to facilitate careful and thoughtful reflection on key issues and a faithful pastoral response that is relevant for every Christian community. Dr. Grcevich has done a real service for church.

DR. JOHN SWINTON, Chair in Divinity and Religious Studies, University of Aberdeen

Dr. Grcevich does not ask us to be perfect, but he does ask us to do what we can. And for most of us, there is much more we can do to welcome people who struggle to find their place among us. This book outlines a realistic, practical approach to inclusion, informed by expert knowledge and experience. It's a must-read for every church leader.

AMY SIMPSON, author of *Troubled Minds: Mental Illness and the Church's Mission*

Dr. Steve Grcevich offers the perfect blend of a psychiatrist's perspective with a ministry leader's heart for the ministry of hope to those with mental health challenges. Not only does he identify the barriers within the church culture for those with mental health issues, but he also provides achievable strategies that empower the church to include those with mental health challenges.

PASTOR BRAD HOEFS, founder of Fresh Hope for Mental Health

This book is a rare find. Dr. Grcevich expertly combines medical information, research, and practical solutions to create a clear path to understanding and inclusion. I predict that well-worn, dog-eared copies will be on the desks of pastors, elders, and Christian educators everywhere. The church will grow in strength and beauty as a result.

KATIE WETHERBEE, learning specialist, Notre Dame College

Mental Health and the Church is an eminently readable and informative book on a topic the church has ignored for far too long. Dr. Grcevich uses his expertise as a child psychiatrist to replace our misconceptions about mental illness and sin with truth. This book holds a place of prominence on my bookshelf, and I will recommend it often in the future.

JOLENE PHILO, author of *Does My Child Have PTSD?* and coauthor of *Every Child Welcome: A Ministry Handbook for Including Kids with Special Needs.*

Too many people with mental illness have been sitting in the back pews of churches, if they are even there at all, for far too long. *Mental Health and the Church* shines a light on a topic that has largely been in the dark. It's educational, biblical, and, thankfully, practical. This book is an answer to prayer.

> **GILLIAN MARCHENKO,** author of *Still Life: A Memoir of Living Fully with Depression*

When I think of people who help churches become safe places for children and adolescents with special needs and hidden disabilities, Dr. Grcevich is the first person who comes to mind. I don't know of anyone in the landscape of today's church who is pioneering these kinds of initiatives and innovative programs. *Mental Health and the Church* will help teachers, counselors, pastors, and caregivers think deeply and biblically about caring for the least of those among us.

> **JONATHAN HOLMES,** pastor of counseling, Parkside Church, and executive director, Fieldstone Counseling

I'm deeply grateful for Dr. Grcevich and his passion for the church to minister well to people impacted by mental illness. There are few trials as painful and few topics as misunderstood. Dr. Grcevich helps crack the code, casting a biblical vision for the body of Christ to minister to people struggling with mental health challenges and to the families who love them.

> **KELLY ROSATI,** vice president, Advocacy for Children, Focus on the Family

This book is long overdue as a truly fresh perspective on an ancient problem. I believe this book will become an industry standard in helping churches minister more compassionately and effectively to children and their families. This is a must-read for all who care about seeing the church meet the needs of many who are hurting and need the gospel.

> **JAMIE RASMUSSEN,** senior pastor, Scottsdale Bible Church

To my father—
for grounding our family in a knowledge of Jesus
and for living a life that served as an example
to me, my wife, and countless others
of someone truly led by the Spirit of God.

To my wife, Denise,
and girls, Leah and Mira—
for their patience and forgiveness
during the times when I failed
to prioritize them over my work or ministry passions.

To Bay Presbyterian Church—
for empowering the people of the church
for the awesome privilege of ministry
and for bestowing their blessing, wisdom, and resources
upon a very young elder with a vision
for a ministry no one else was doing.

To the board and staff of Key Ministry, past and present—
this book is the product of our collective work and experience.
All of you had a part.
I'm grateful that God provided me the opportunity
to serve alongside each of you.

Contents

Foreword

Before having children, I read eight books on parenting. Clearly, I was an anxious overachiever who wanted to raise "the perfect family."

I am the third of four kids in the Swindoll family. My dad has been in Christian ministry for more than fifty years. I stopped counting years ago how many books he's written. Sundays were sacred in our home; Christian education, midweek Bible studies, and weekend retreats were central to the rhythm of our lives.

Many in Christian ministry would assume our family life was ideal because it appeared that way. But things aren't always as they appear, are they? What people outside our home never saw was my mother's struggles with deep depression, attempted suicide, a childhood history of profound abuse, and the scars of emotional detachment. My mother suffered in silence with severe migraines, chronic pain, and pervasive anxiety due to the relentless expectations of public ministry. There was no intentional hiding or some secret sin, but the stigma attached to mental and emotional distress only exacerbated our family's suffering in silence.

Just as the body is a system that functions with countless moving parts, the family is a dynamic system. If the physical body is compromised, it affects the functioning of the whole body. In most church communities, we do a great job providing support for those struggling with physical compromise, yet when there is mention of the need for support related to mental and emotional compromise, the response is often offensive and judgmental.

I know this not just from my family of origin, but from personal experience with my children. When my daughter was in middle school, she began cutting and drinking, and she wanted nothing to do with the church and became increasingly defiant. When I sought help from those in the church, we were met with a "fixit" mentality: do more "Christian" things like pray and read Scripture. The most painful part was the judgment and rejection. While none of these people lived in our home, they seemed to have all the answers about living in our home. At one point, I felt like giving up on the church all together.

For years, my confidence in trusting Christ as my Savior rested on my knowledge of the Bible, the evidence that he had transformed my thoughts and actions, and my capacity for withstanding adversity. He promises us strength in the storms, a refuge of hope when trials prevail, and a peace that surpasses all understanding. Herein lies one of the most pervasive misunderstandings regarding mental illness: that God spares this kind of pain and suffering from those with deep and abiding faith. All too often, the assumption in the church is that those who continue to suffer from mental illness lack sufficient faith.

Topics like mental illness, abuse, and chronic physical and emotional stress are not popular in the church, which is one of the biggest tragedies of all. My faith in Jesus Christ is thoroughly authentic. What is just as true is my diagnosis of ADHD, anxiety, PTSD, chronic pain, structural abnormalities, and a genetic mutation that causes a greater propensity for depression. One cannot separate out these challenges; they are pieces of a whole person that require spiritual, emotional, physical, and therapeutic support. How I long for the church to understand we are whole people made of many moving parts—some parts are healthy, and others aren't.

One of the first people to comprehend this truth was Dr. Steve Grcevich. In 2004, he reached out and offered help with my son's disabling conditions. When my daughter was suicidal, he referred us to a program we began to follow. Through his support, her symptoms of anxiety and depression were dramatically reversed. I am forever grateful that a Christian friend helped save my son and daughter's lives.

Steve's book is a work of monumental, transformative value. I have learned more about my sinful nature, the truths of Christ, and what it truly means to be a Christian as I have found help and healing through our suffering. My daughter is happily married, pursuing a graduate degree, and utilizing the many gifts God has given her. My son with disabilities may never read or comprehend his grandfather's written or spoken word about the Christian life. Yet he will never forget how his Bubba authentically embraced and loved him—because my son is loved by his Bubba as Christ loves you and me.

There are countless others with less obvious disabilities than those that affect the Swindoll family. But the truth is, we need one another. We need to embrace the whole person and not segment lives according to what we're comfortable discussing.

If you want to live a full Christian life, you must become comfortable with those whom Christ embraced. I have to ask:

- Have you offered encouragement to a parent of a child struggling with self-control?
- Have you sat with someone who was overwhelmed with anxiety?
- Have you comforted a parent or a spouse of someone who has attempted or committed suicide?
- Have you taken the time to consider how Christ will become real to those who struggle to form relationships with other people?

If you are led to honor Christ through helping your church to care for people with mental illness—the most common type of disability in the US—I strongly suggest you start with this book. The ideas reflect a heart of enormous compassion, a mind of extensive knowledge, and an understanding of extraordinary grace. Your perspective on welcoming those who are typically overlooked and undervalued will change if you integrate these principles into your church program.

If you want to change the world, begin with those who are hurting and watch God's magnificent work begin to unfold in and around you.

Colleen Swindoll-Thompson,
director of Reframing Ministries,
Insight for Living

PART ONE

UNDERSTANDING THE PROBLEM

ONE

The Disconnect

Most days, I live in two different worlds—my professional world and my church world. The children and families I meet in my professional world are often strangely absent from my life at church. Allow me to explain.

I'm a physician. Since completing my residency training in general psychiatry and an additional fellowship in child psychiatry nearly thirty years ago, I've practiced as a child and adolescent psychiatrist. I've participated in research, studying medications commonly prescribed to children and teens with mental health disorders. I teach medical students and residents. Much of my work takes place in a group practice based in a Cleveland suburb. I typically spend my days evaluating and treating kids who struggle with the full range of emotional and behavioral problems common among kids growing up in twenty-first-century America. Anxiety disorders and attention deficit/hyperactivity disorder (ADHD) are the two most common conditions we treat in our practice, but I also see lots of kids with mood disorders, autism spectrum disorders, obsessive-compulsive disorder (OCD), learning disorders, and post-traumatic stress disorder.

In my professional world, I enjoy helping kids and families apply new strategies to help them live happier and more productive lives. But I frequently go home with the knowledge that the families I see in my practice are unlikely to get what they most need for their long-term peace and well-being.

In my church world, our family regularly gathers with other like-minded families, and we seek to honor and worship Jesus Christ. My wife, two daughters, and I have been blessed to attend a church where we've experienced excellent teaching, received encouragement and support for pursuing ministry interests, and formed lifelong friendships through our involvement in a small group.

There's a big disconnect between the two worlds I live in each week. Perhaps you feel it too if you're a church leader, a mental health professional, someone with personal experience of mental illness, or a family member of someone with mental illness. What's the disconnect? *The families I meet through my work as a child and adolescent psychiatrist are far less likely than other families in our community to be actively involved in a local church.*

This reality is a tragic departure from Jesus' plan for his church. The families I see in my practice need to hear the gospel message proclaimed just as much as my family does. They need good teaching, service opportunities, and small group community just as much as my family does. They have gifts and talents intended by God for the benefit of the church that result in the church being incomplete without them.

My intention in writing this book is to bridge the gap between my two worlds and make it easier for individuals and families affected by mental illness to fully participate in the life of a local church.

My eyes were opened to the need twenty years ago when I was serving on our church's elder board. The children's ministry director came to one of our meetings to discuss challenges facing some of our church's most committed families. Several families had adopted children from orphanages in Russia and Bulgaria after the fall of the Iron Curtain. Many of the adopted children arrived in America with complex emotional, behavioral, and developmental disabilities. Their families struggled to stay involved with the church. The severity of aggressive behavior, meltdowns, and impulsiveness demonstrated by the children prevented their families from attending Sunday morning worship services and hindered their ability to maintain their volunteer commitments or small group involvement.

As I listened to our children's ministry director discuss the needs of our church's adoptive families, the challenges she was describing were like those of families seeking help through our practice. I began routinely asking parents of the kids I was treating—kids with common conditions, including ADHD, anxiety, autism, depression, and other mood disorders—how their child's condition impacted their ability to attend church. Their answers made my jaw drop. I was struck by the hurt and disappointment described by parents following unsuccessful attempts to attend church together as a family.

I began inviting families to our church who lived within a reasonable distance and were comfortable with our theologically conservative beliefs. Over time, I made mental notes when families in other parts of the city described positive experiences of church. I encouraged families who were struggling to stay involved with their church to connect their leaders with our church's family ministry team if their congregation was interested in getting help. God began to put a larger plan in motion.

LOOKING FOR ANSWERS

One of my frustrations as a child psychiatrist practicing in the mid-1990s was the lack of published research on treatments for common emotional and behavioral challenges in children. I stumbled into clinical research because I wanted to know how to more effectively treat the kids I was seeing in our practice. Despite having published only one research paper at that point in my career, I received one of the first three research grants for Adderall, which became the most popular prescription medication for treating children and adults with ADHD in the United States.

My involvement in the Adderall research led to numerous speaking and teaching invitations over the next few years—more than I could handle! When invited to speak, I would mention the services our church was providing to families with a broad range of needs, including mental health needs. Requests for help began pouring in from churches across the country. The physicians and mental health professionals I met through my presentations recognized the need among their families for support in attending church.

OUR RESPONSE: KEY MINISTRY

A core group of pastoral staff and leaders from my church formed Key Ministry in late 2002 in response to requests coming in from churches around the country for assistance in serving families of children with significant emotional, behavioral, or developmental challenges. The language we incorporated into our original mission statement was "to build the body of Christ by empowering churches to minister to families of children with hidden disabilities."

At the time when Key Ministry was launched, many churches had launched ministries to support the inclusion of persons with physical disabilities. A smaller group of churches had started special needs ministries that served children and adults with intellectual or developmental disabilities. For families of children and teens with less obvious disabilities, support at church was virtually nonexistent.

Our ministry used the term *hidden disabilities* to describe significant emotional, behavioral, developmental, or neurologic conditions lacking outwardly apparent physical symptoms and set about the work of helping churches minister to people with these conditions. Mental health conditions aside, hidden disabilities that often interfere with a child's ability to participate in worship services or church activities include:

- dyslexia or other learning disorders
- communication disorders

- neurodevelopmental complications associated with trauma or neglect
- brain injuries resulting from physical trauma, epilepsy, or stroke.

We never intended that our ministry would focus exclusively on mental health inclusion. Most of the requests we receive for training and consultation services result from ministry challenges with kids with severe intellectual or developmental disabilities that fall within our definition of special needs. We work alongside many fine ministry leaders and organizations that have blossomed in recent years to help churches serve the special needs population, and we're encouraged by the progress churches have made in special needs ministry. Unfortunately, we've made little or no progress in helping churches develop an inclusion strategy for children, adults, and families affected by the most common disabilities in the United States—mental illness.

According to the National Institute of Mental Health and the US Centers for Disease Control, approximately 4.5 million children between the ages of eight and fifteen have a mental health disorder at any given time. It is estimated that 21.4 percent of America's twenty million teenagers will experience an episode of mental illness categorized as "severe" by the time they turn eighteen. The Substance Abuse and Mental Health Services Administration (SAMHSA) estimated that in 2015, 17.9 percent of the adult population, or 43.4 million American adults, had experienced at least one mental illness.[1] Combining the child and adult populations, *more than fifty million Americans today experience at least one diagnosable mental health disorder on any given day*!

Let's look more closely at some of the experiences of children and teens in the US who are affected by mental illness:

- 11 percent of children ages four to seventeen in 2011 had ever received an ADHD diagnosis.[2]

- 8–12 percent of teens experience anxiety disorders; less than one in five receive any treatment—psychotherapy or medication.[3]
- 16.1 million adults (6.7 percent of all US adults) experienced an episode of major depression during 2015.[4]
- 18.1 percent of adults experienced an anxiety disorder during 2015.[5]
- Suicide is the second leading cause of death in the United States (following unintentional injury) among individuals ages fifteen to thirty-four.[6]

An emerging body of research seeks to quantify the challenges associated with attending church among families impacted by mental illness. In 2014, LifeWay Research released the results of a study conducted in partnership with Focus on the Family that surveyed Protestant pastors, Protestant adults identified with mental illness, and family members of Protestants with mental illness on the associations between mental illness and faith practice. The results were published in the "Study of Acute Mental Illness and Christian Faith" research report.[7] Key findings of the study included:

- While 23 percent of pastors indicated they've struggled personally with mental illness, only 12 percent were formally diagnosed (p. 18).
- While 56 percent of pastors strongly agree that local churches have a responsibility to provide resources and support to individuals with mental illness and their families (p. 32) and 68 percent of pastors indicate their church provides care for the mentally ill or their families by maintaining lists of experts for referral, only 28 percent of family members reported the resources and supports were available through their church (p. 35).
- 66 percent of pastors discuss mental illness in sermons or large group messages once a year, rarely, or never (p. 37).

The study points to an enormous disconnect between the perceptions of pastors regarding the support offered through churches to families impacted by mental illness and the experiences of families seeking support. The study suggests mental illness remains a topic that too many pastors are reluctant to discuss with their congregations. It also suggests that many pastors who might benefit from mental health evaluation and treatment either lack the health care benefits or financial resources to obtain care for themselves, don't know where to go to access care, or choose not to seek care because of the stigma associated with mental illness in many denominations and local churches.

The LifeWay report builds on research from Baylor University described in an article titled "Demon or Disorder: A Survey of Attitudes toward Mental Illness and the Church."[8] The Baylor investigators found that three in ten attendees who sought help from their church for themselves or a family member for a mental health condition reported "negative interactions" that were counterproductive to treatment. Commonly reported negative interactions included abandonment by the church, church leaders equating mental illness with the work of demons, and suggestions from church leaders that their mental disorder was the result of personal sin. Women were significantly more likely than men to report having their mental illness dismissed by the church and/or receiving advice to not take psychiatric medication.

The church has a big problem. The Baylor study suggests it is not uncommon for established families to leave their local congregations and not come back after seeking care and support from the church when a family member is affected by mental illness. In a later chapter, we'll look at research examining the perceptions of adults who don't regularly attend worship services about attitudes regarding mental illness in the church. Hundreds upon hundreds of messages and comments directed to our ministry support the notion that church leaders have a well-deserved reputation for shooting our wounded when Christians seek care and support for mental health concerns.

Far too many pastors, church leaders, and attendees within our Christian subculture demonstrate an insufficient understanding of the nature of mental illness and struggle to respond to those affected in a manner that demonstrates compassion and concern and promotes spiritual growth. Fewer still possess a basic understanding of how the experience of mental illness impacts the ability of affected children, adults, and their families to participate in worship services, small groups, educational programming, and service activities through which spiritual growth takes place.

Why does the church struggle to minister to persons affected by mental illness? One possible explanation is that many Christians find it hard to integrate mental illness into our understanding of the relationship between our bodies, minds, and souls.

The church has made great strides in ministry with persons with *physical* disabilities. Joni Eareckson Tada has built a marvelous organization (Joni and Friends) that provides outreach to families affected by disability around the world.[9] Joni and Friends disciples people affected by disability to exercise their gifts in their churches and communities and prods the church to include persons with disabilities into the fabric of their worship, fellowship, and outreach. Its Family Retreats ministry offers a place for special needs families to be encouraged and rejuvenated in a camp setting. Its Wheels for the World ministry provides refurbished wheelchairs and the hope of the gospel to persons in need in all corners of the world. Its Christian Institute on Disability plays an important role in promoting life, human dignity, and the value of all persons, pointing people to a deeper understanding of how our faith should inform ministry with persons with disabilities.

Scripture clearly describes how bodily illness is a consequence of life in a fallen world. The Bible contains many stories of Jesus' healing of the sick during his earthly ministry. Jesus gave very clear instructions to his followers about the need to include persons with disabilities in the life of the church so that the church reflects the nature of his kingdom: "When you give a banquet, invite the poor, the crippled, the lame, the blind, and you will be blessed. Although they cannot repay you, you will be repaid at the resurrection of the righteous" (Luke 14:13–14).

Jesus challenged common understandings of disability and made clear that disability is a means through which Christ builds his kingdom:

> As he went along, he saw a man blind from birth. His disciples asked him, "Rabbi, who sinned, this man or his parents, that he was born blind?"
>
> "Neither this man nor his parents sinned," said Jesus, "but this happened so that the works of God might be displayed in him."
>
> *John 9:1–3*

Scripture contains a surprising number of descriptions of people with signs and symptoms associated with mental illness. Psalm 102 describes a man with weight loss, appetite disturbance, sleep disturbance, and social isolation (common signs and symptoms of depression), who turns to God seeking mercy for himself and for his nation:

> Hear my prayer, LORD;
> > let my cry for help come to you.
> Do not hide your face from me
> > when I am in distress.
> Turn your ear to me;
> > when I call, answer me quickly.
>
> For my days vanish like smoke;
> > my bones burn like glowing embers.
> My heart is blighted and withered like grass;
> > I forget to eat my food.
> In my distress I groan aloud
> > and am reduced to skin and bones.
> I am like a desert owl,

like an owl among the ruins.
I lie awake; I have become
like a bird alone on a roof.
All day long my enemies taunt me;
those who rail against me use my name as a curse.
For I eat ashes as my food
and mingle my drink with tears
because of your great wrath,
for you have taken me up and thrown me aside.
My days are like the evening shadow;
I wither away like grass.

Psalm 102:1–11

The harmful spirit that tormented King Saul in 1 Samuel would likely be characterized as mental illness by a twenty-first-century observer.[10] The Spirit of the Lord departed from Saul after his disobedience led God to reject him as Israel's king. In 1 Samuel 16, David is called to the royal court to use his skills as a musician to relieve Saul's distress:

Now the Spirit of the LORD had departed from Saul, and an evil spirit from the LORD tormented him.

Saul's attendants said to him, "See, an evil spirit from God is tormenting you. Let our lord command his servants here to search for someone who can play the lyre. He will play when the evil spirit from God comes on you, and you will feel better."

So Saul said to his attendants, "Find someone who plays well and bring him to me."

One of the servants answered, "I have seen a son of Jesse of Bethlehem who knows how to play the lyre. He is a brave man and a warrior. He speaks well and is a fine-looking man. And the LORD is with him."

Then Saul sent messengers to Jesse and said, "Send me your son David, who is with the sheep." So Jesse took a donkey loaded with bread, a skin of wine and a young goat and sent them with his son David to Saul.

David came to Saul and entered his service. Saul liked him very much, and David became one of his armor-bearers. Then Saul sent word to Jesse, saying, "Allow David to remain in my service, for I am pleased with him."

Whenever the spirit from God came on Saul, David would take up his lyre and play. Then relief would come to Saul; he would feel better, and the evil spirit would leave him.

1 Samuel 16:14–23

King Nebuchadnezzar is the most famous person identified with boanthropy—a rare form of psychosis in which a person develops the delusional belief that they are a cow or an ox. In the book of Daniel, we read, "Immediately what had been said about Nebuchadnezzar was fulfilled. He was driven away from people and ate grass like the ox. His body was drenched with the dew of heaven until his hair grew like the feathers of an eagle and his nails like the claws of a bird" (Daniel 4:33).

In the opening chapter of 2 Corinthians, the apostle Paul describes ministry troubles that led him to experience deep despair. The apostle recognizes two useful purposes in his suffering. Paul's despair led him to increase his reliance on God while enhancing his ability to comfort other believers during their time of suffering:

Praise be to the God and Father of our Lord Jesus Christ, the Father of compassion and the God of all comfort, who comforts us in all our troubles, so that we can comfort those in any trouble with the comfort we ourselves receive from God. For just as we share abundantly in the sufferings of Christ, so also our comfort abounds through Christ. If we are distressed, it is for your comfort and salvation; if we are comforted, it is for your comfort, which produces in you patient endurance of the same sufferings we suffer. And our hope for you is firm, because we

know that just as you share in our sufferings, so also you share
in our comfort.

We do not want you to be uninformed, brothers and sisters,
about the troubles we experienced in the province of Asia. We
were under great pressure, far beyond our ability to endure, so
that we despaired of life itself. Indeed, we felt we had received
the sentence of death. But this happened that we might not rely
on ourselves but on God, who raises the dead.

2 Corinthians 1:3–9

Yet while the church is making progress in addressing the needs of
persons with *physical* disabilities, many pastors and leaders in the church
struggle to fully integrate *mental illness* into their theology and praxis.
One reason for this lack of integration is that while physical illness
often appears unrelated to that person's moral choices and behaviors,
the relationship is less clear with mental illness and disability. From the
founding of the church, pastors and theologians have wrestled with the
concept of free will—the extent to which we make choices free from
coercion. The apostle Paul wrestles with this in Romans 7.

I do not understand what I do. For what I want to do I do not
do, but what I hate I do. And if I do what I do not want to do,
I agree that the law is good. As it is, it is no longer I myself who
do it, but it is sin living in me. For I know that good itself does
not dwell in me, that is, in my sinful nature. For I have the desire
to do what is good, but I cannot carry it out. For I do not do the
good I want to do, but the evil I do not want to do—this I keep
on doing. Now if I do what I do not want to do, it is no longer I
who do it, but it is sin living in me that does it.

Romans 7:15–20

Mental illness forces us to consider an individual's ability to make
moral judgments based on a notion of right and wrong and their

capacity to refrain from actions and behaviors identified as sinful in Scripture. We wrestle with the extent to which mental illness mitigates their accountability for their actions, a capacity often referred to as "moral agency." One reason the church struggles to achieve a common understanding of how best to minister to children and adults with mental illness stems from ongoing disagreement about the extent to which individuals can control their own behavior—and rightly so! This is a complex issue requiring the synthesis of a biblical understanding of human personhood, medical and psychological research, and practices developed from those understandings, ideas, and beliefs.

Parents who come to our practice often ask me if their children can control the behaviors that led them to seek help. They frequently demonstrate a propensity for "all-or-nothing" thinking in their understanding of problem behaviors. They seem to believe that children are either *always* or *never* able to control their actions.

A more accurate understanding of self-control in persons with mental health conditions is that they possess *some* ability to manage their actions and emotions. They're capable of self-control, but they may need to devote more mental effort and cognitive resources to maintaining control than children or adults of comparable age and intelligence. Their capacity for self-control is often diminished when they are involved in activities and environments where their brains need to devote more cognitive capacity to processing new information or sensory input—environments like church, for example. A person's capacity for self-control often decreases as the number of distractions they encounter or the number or complexity of the decisions they need to make increases. When we say that children or young adults "need structure," we are describing environments that simplify the cognitive demands to which a person is exposed so they will retain capacity to make good choices and decisions.

Churches may be more accepting of special needs ministry because church leaders recognize the diminished capacity for "moral agency" among persons with more profound intellectual or developmental disabilities. We don't believe they bear any personal responsibility for their conditions—like the man described in John 9 with congenital blindness who was healed by Jesus. The issue of personal responsibility is less clear with mental illness.

Many churches have implemented effective ministry models for welcoming and including children and adults with physical disabilities. Thousands of churches have taken steps to make their facilities more accessible—providing wheelchair ramps, elevators, restrooms, amplification equipment or interpreters for persons with hearing impairments, and, in some instances, nurses to assist members and attendees who have significant medical needs.

We have excellent ministry models for serving children and adults with "special needs." Many churches offer a modified Christian education curriculum and provide volunteer or staff support in the form of "buddies" for children or teens who require individualized attention. The Tim Tebow Foundation has popularized church-sponsored proms as outreach events to teens and adults with intellectual disabilities and their families.

Many factors have fueled the expansion of church-based special needs ministries over the last two decades. Successful special needs ministries were started by several large, influential churches (McLean Bible Church, Stonebriar Church, and Lakewood Church) after a child or grandchild of a senior pastor was identified with a significant intellectual or developmental disability. Leaders spoke publicly of the need, and substantial resources were committed to the ministry. Large increases in the number of children diagnosed with autism and enhanced public awareness have spurred demand for special needs ministry. Thanks to medical advances, more children born very prematurely are surviving with special needs, and persons with chromosomal abnormalities and genetic disorders are living longer. Adoption and foster care ministries have brought more children with special needs to families already involved in the church. The rapid proliferation of social media and improvements in technology have made special needs ministry training and resources more accessible and affordable to church staff and volunteers.

Why haven't we seen a similar proliferation of ministry promoting evangelism and outreach to families impacted by mental illness? We have a well-known pastor and his wife (Rick and Kay Warren) who have spoken publicly about their family's experience of mental illness following the suicide of their son Matthew. Saddleback Church has hosted several large conferences to increase understanding and awareness of mental illness among church leaders. Far more families in ministry—and the public at large—are affected by mental illness than any other category of disability. The technology and social media resources available to support ministry are no different for mental health than for special needs.

I believe there are three reasons that intentional mental health ministry hasn't taken off in America:

- Mental illness is stigmatized in many of our churches in ways that other disabilities aren't. The stigma may be greater in churches and denominations most inclined to pursue evangelism and outreach.
- The term "mental illness" is used to describe a very broad range of conditions affecting thinking, perception, mood, emotions, and behavior. The typical pastor or ministry leader may have *some* knowledge of the signs and symptoms of *some* conditions, but an in-depth understanding of how the attributes of common mental health disorders impact church participation or spiritual growth is extremely rare in my experience.
- We haven't had a commonly accepted ministry model for mental health outreach and inclusion.

Our Key Ministry team came to recognize that existing models of disability ministry in churches—designed to serve children and adults with intellectual, developmental, and physical disabilities—don't work for people who have common mental health conditions. Mike Woods is an expert in behavioral intervention for children with autism spectrum disorders, the father of three young adult sons with autism, and the former director of a large and vital special needs ministry at First Baptist Church in Orlando, Florida. Mike posed the following question in response to an article from our ministry on the need for mental health inclusion at church: "Would I expect to find a person with mental health struggles (depression, bipolar disorder, schizophrenia) to be part of our disability ministry at First Baptist Orlando? No. For me, mental illness is a separate... and much needed... ministry within the church."[11]

For the last three years, my principal "ministry" role has been to develop a model for mental health inclusion adaptable by churches of all sizes, denominations, and organizational styles. This book describes the current state of our inclusion model. I expect this model will continue to evolve as churches acquire more experience in ministry with families impacted by mental illness. The model draws on the accumulated experience of our team members, who have been serving churches since 2002, as well as on the experience I've gained from thirty years of caring for thousands of kids and families with a broad range of mental health conditions.

In the coming chapters, we'll take a closer look at how functional demands within the primary environments where ministry takes place, along with select features of church culture, represent significant barriers to church attendance and spiritual growth for those with common mental health conditions. God has placed a burden on our ministry team to champion the full inclusion of kids, teens, and adults with mental illness and their families in our churches.

In this first part of the book, we'll consider the attributes of common mental health conditions that make church participation difficult for affected persons and their families. We'll explore why persons with mental illness don't fit into traditional ministry models and why their needs often go undetected in churches. And I will introduce seven common barriers to church participation for children, teens, and adults with common mental health conditions and their families, as well as seven broad ministry strategies for churches to consider implementing as part of a mental health inclusion initiative.

In the second part of the book, I'll explore how the inclusion strategies introduced in part 1 can be applied across your church's ministry activities and environments to support full integration of children and adults impacted by mental illness and their families into every activity and experience offered by the church. These chapters are shorter and are filled with practical ideas and suggestions. Feel free to jump around if you'd like, focusing on the conditions that are of greatest concern to you and your church.

I'll conclude by providing you with practical resources for use in a mental health inclusion initiative in your church. You will be invited to share in an ongoing dialogue with brothers and sisters in Christ with a specific call to mental health ministry and connect with others serving faithfully throughout the disability ministry movement.

I'm deeply encouraged by the emerging movement of pastors, ministry leaders, professionals, volunteers, and family members who are responding to God's call to share the love of Christ and his message of salvation with persons affected by mental illness. The work that God has placed before us has the potential to impact millions of individuals and families who have all too frequently been excluded from local churches. Together, we can make a difference.

---- | TWO | ----

A Different Type
of Disability

When we launched Key Ministry, one of the very first tasks we took on was to identify and connect with church leaders, ministries, family members, and professionals with common interests and passions. As we began networking, we found that our ministry goals naturally resonated with a burgeoning community of disability ministry leaders. We were welcomed into their fellowship, but quickly recognized that ministry with children and teens with significant emotional or behavior challenges fell beyond their understanding of disability or special needs ministry. At the same time, we were learning from leaders in children's, student, and family ministries that kids with mental health challenges often struggled with the standard church programming offered to children and youth.

Our interest in mental health inclusion led to a bit of an identity crisis for our ministry. We have firmly had one foot planted in the children's/family ministry community and one foot in the disability ministry community in recent years. Key Ministry has identified a need that doesn't fit into the established programming categories—the established church models of "disability ministry" or "special needs" ministry—common throughout the American church. Ministry leaders serving in the trenches have been quick to recognize the need for new approaches for serving kids who struggle with their thinking, emotions, and behavior. One of our greatest challenges has been to find the right language for communicating the needs of the kids and families we serve in a way that helps church leaders and families respond to the call for a new kind of ministry.

As a physician who specializes in child and adolescent psychiatry, I recognize that the conditions I treat among my patients are significant *disabilities* in that they interfere with participation in major life activities. Yet the families I serve in my practice generally aren't viewed as beneficiaries of a traditional disability ministry in a church. Why? Because their conditions don't fit within the common understanding of disability in the church.

Let's start unraveling this problem by clearly defining the terms *mental illness* and *disability*.

Federal law defines an individual with a disability as "a person who has a mental or physical impairment that substantially limits one or more major life activities; a record of such an impairment; or being regarded as having such an impairment."[1] This definition is very relevant for our discussion because the law specifies what qualifies as an "impairment"—something that substantially limits one or more major life activities. Note, too, that the law adds, "An impairment that substantially limits one major life activity *need not limit other major life activities* in order to be considered a disability" (emphasis mine). My point is that the impairment or illness can limit just one life activity. Examples from my practice include bright teenagers with the inattentive subtype of ADHD who experience difficulties with time management, planning, organization, and work completion that greatly affect academic performance but have little impact on friendships, family relationships, or extracurricular activities. *Note: Readers familiar with the diagnostic criteria for ADHD know that the disorder must be present in two or more settings. Given the volume of academic work expected of most high schoolers, home represents the second setting.*

A pastor I treated for agoraphobia serves as another example. He was prone to incapacitating panic attacks when he would get up to preach before hundreds of people gathered for weekend worship services, but was relatively symptom-free everywhere else.

Disability law also recognizes that a person is still considered to have an impairment even when their conditions are episodic or in remission. This is an important distinction because many of the people we're talking about with mental health conditions who are struggling to initiate or maintain involvement in the church experience *episodic* disability.

The National Alliance on Mental Illness (NAMI) defines mental illness as "a condition that affects a person's thinking, feeling or mood."[2] The *Diagnostic and Statistical Manual of Mental Disorders* (*DSM-5*) provides the following definition for a mental disorder: "A mental disorder is a syndrome characterized by clinically significant disturbance in an individual's cognition, emotion regulation, or behavior that reflects a dysfunction in the psychological, biological, or developmental processes underlying mental functioning."[3]

The complete *DSM-5* definition emphasizes that mental disorders are usually associated with "significant distress or disability in social, occupational, or other important activities." If you've read this far in the book, you likely consider church participation and spiritual growth to be "important activities." The bottom line is that a mental health condition resulting in little impact on academic or work performance would still be considered a disability for someone who considers spiritual development to be a *major life activity* if that condition were to significantly interfere with their ability to attend church and exercise their faith.

A NEW WAY OF THINKING ABOUT DISABILITY

Is a disability still considered a disability if a person is disabled some but not all the time? That question was the original title for this chapter.

Upon further reflection, I thought it might scare off potential readers who would skim through the table of contents. Nevertheless, the question points to three important attributes of mental illness that depart significantly from our current understanding of disability in the church. These attributes of mental illness help us recognize why attending church is often difficult for children and adults with common mental health conditions and inform the strategies we develop to involve them in the full range of activities offered through the local church:

- *Episodic.* Many common mental health conditions are characterized by symptoms that come and go. The need for support—and the types of support needed—may vary greatly from year to year or even from week to week.

- *Hidden.* The presence of a mental health-related disability is often difficult to quantify or measure—even for highly trained professionals! Children and adults with mental health conditions who come to church often try very hard to keep their disability hidden from church staff and volunteers. Many seek to avoid any special treatment or supports that might single them out as "different." The stigma connected to mental illness that is still prevalent in the Christian community causes many to keep their struggles to themselves.

- *Situation-specific.* Signs of mental health-related disability frequently emerge from the unique demands and cultural expectations persons face in the situations and environments they enter throughout the week. A person with a mental health condition associated with sensory processing differences may have no difficulty sitting through a Bible study or sermon, but he or she may experience profound distress if the worship team tests the upper limits of performance on their sound system during a Sunday morning service. We'll explore this attribute in the greatest depth because several of our proposed inclusion strategies involve recognizing how our processes for outreach and assimilation, the physical qualities of the spaces where ministry takes place, and the nature of the activities we engage in when gathered together present challenges for children and adults with mental illness.

Let's take a closer look at how these attributes impact the day-to-day functioning of persons affected by mental illness.

Some people with mental health disorders—even serious ones—may experience extended periods in which they are relatively symptom-free. Consider a teen or adult who experiences recurrent episodes of major depression. They may function at a high level for many years. They may even serve as pastors or in other key leadership positions in the church. As they become symptomatic, they may have trouble falling asleep or staying asleep. They may struggle with lack of concentration or forgetfulness. They withdraw from activities and relationships they've enjoyed for years.

The man who attends your early morning Bible study is absent for weeks at a time without explanation. The teen who has been a regular at youth group shows no interest in signing up for the annual weekend retreat. The woman you've served alongside in your church's homeless ministry doesn't respond to your voice mails or text invitations for coffee. As their episodes progress, they may have to take time away from work or school and may lose contact with friends from church as they struggle to maintain social obligations. Some may struggle with suicidal thoughts or spend time in a hospital if they see suicide as a viable strategy for finding relief from their mental anguish.

Or consider a teen with bipolar disorder who may go for months or years without symptoms but quickly transitions into episodes of diminished judgment and capacity for self-control, often accompanied by grandiose delusions, euphoria, agitation, irritability, and hallucinations. Some children and adults with anxiety disorders may function at a high level for weeks or months—as long as they're avoiding situations that trigger incapacitating fear. When a trigger occurs, it may produce overwhelming anxiety. John Madden, the beloved football commentator, Hall of Fame coach, and namesake of one of America's most popular video games, has struggled with intense anxiety later in life. His claustrophobia (fear of confined places) formed the basis of his well-known fear of flying. He became famous for his reliance on ground transportation when traveling to games, and for the last twenty years of his broadcast career, he traveled the country in a customized bus known as "the Madden Cruiser."

The hidden nature of most mental health-related disabilities often leads to situations at church in which volunteers and church staff with good intentions inadvertently cause embarrassment or discomfort. Church greeters, for example, have no way of knowing whether a first-time attender they're welcoming has social anxiety disorder and will spend the entire church service ruminating on their fears that they're making a bad impression on every person they've casually met since passing through the front door. Most Sunday school teachers wouldn't know whether the boy sitting in the front row has dyslexia or why he ran out of class crying after they asked each kid in the room to take turns reading from the Bible. The chairman of the elder board may not recognize that the aggressive behavior of the senior pastor's adopted son during the recent domestic mission trip is an indication of past trauma as opposed to bad parenting or the pastor's failure to provide his family with appropriate discipline or spiritual leadership.

Churches are less likely to provide much-needed support to members and attendees during periods of serious illness or disability when their conditions aren't readily visible. When someone is confined to a bed in a hospital or at home recovering from surgery for a broken leg or knee replacement, the need for an encouraging word or help with a few meals is eminently clear.

Several years ago, I authored a blog post a few days after the airing of a segment on CBS's *60 Minutes* that explored the crisis many families experience in finding care for children with severe mental illness. A mother shared this illustration to describe the differences in the support their family received from their church following two different episodes of illness:

> My daughter, when she was thirteen, was hit by a car and fortunately was fine, except for a very bad broken leg. The church organized a brigade of casserole makers, the neighbors brought casseroles, friends, families, everybody. Six months before that, Christina had spent two months on a psychiatric ward, and we had no casseroles. And I'm not blaming the church or the neighbors or anything . . . because of the stigma, we didn't tell people.[4]

Because we have well-researched and widely accepted diagnostic tests to identify the presence of serious medical illnesses, no one questions whether a friend with positive biopsy results and a visible mass on an MRI scan is experiencing cancer; whether a coworker with fatigue, thirst, and elevated blood sugar has diabetes; or whether a child who loses consciousness and exhibits characteristically abnormal patterns of brain-wave activity on an EEG has epilepsy.

Unfortunately, in the last half of the second decade of the twenty-first century, that's not true when it comes to mental illness. Because of the challenges in measuring the functions of the human brain at a cellular and molecular level, psychiatry is far behind other medical specialties and subspecialties in developing objective tests to establish diagnoses. While neuroimaging and genetic studies have greatly contributed to our rapidly expanding understanding of mental illness, our current technology lacks the sensitivity (ability to detect the condition in question) and specificity required to conclusively diagnose common mental health conditions in individuals.

The absence of objective tests to unequivocally establish the presence of mental health conditions has led many church leaders to question the validity of mental health diagnoses and express suspicion toward mental health professionals. This suspicion fueled a movement in the world of Christian counseling often referred to as biblical or "nouthetic" counseling, which attributes the presence of mental illness to personal sin.[5] While other influential leaders in the Christian counseling movement are less skeptical of the existence of mental illness or the potential benefits of available mental health treatments, the influence of Jay Adams and other nouthetic counselors has contributed to some of the stigma associated with mental illness in many churches today. We'll explore the origins of the stigma connected to mental illness in the church and strategies for addressing the stigma in a subsequent chapter.

MENTAL ILLNESS AS A PRODUCT OF THE CULTURE

A frequent criticism of my fellow medical and mental health professionals is that we're too quick to attach diagnostic labels to common patterns of emotion and behavior. Let's take a few minutes to consider how our larger culture is contributing to the proliferation of mental illness.

Several years ago, a cartoon made the rounds on social media. This cartoon depicted a bird, a monkey, a penguin, an elephant, a seal, and a dog, among other animals. One version had in the row of animals a goldfish in a bowl that was set on top of a stump in a field with a tree in the background, facing an educator seated behind a big desk. The educator demanded for the sake of fairness that *all* animals needed to take the *same* test: climbing a large tree looming in the background, something that was clearly impossible for a *goldfish*.[6]

The cartoon was intended to illustrate the frustration that many kids, parents, and teachers experience when they run up against inflexible educational standards and standardized tests that fail to account for a student's full range of gifts and abilities. This is a common frustration among the families that pass through our practice.

Mental illness is proliferating because the demands of life are proliferating. In the quarter century since I completed my child psychiatry training, I've witnessed a steep increase in the numbers of families seeking treatment for children with symptoms of ADHD or anxiety.

We'll look at ADHD as an illustration of the relationship between culture and mental illness. A study published in 2014 reveals that the prevalence of ADHD among children and teens dramatically changed between 2003 and 2011:

- A parent-reported history of ADHD increased by 42 percent from 2003 to 2011.
- Prevalence of a history of ADHD, current ADHD, medicated ADHD, and moderate to severe ADHD increased significantly from 2007 estimates.
- Prevalence of medicated ADHD increased by 28 percent from 2007 to 2011.
- Approximately two million more US children/adolescents aged four to seventeen years had been diagnosed with ADHD in 2011 compared to 2003.[7]

Why have we seen such a rapid increase in the prevalence of these conditions? In the case of ADHD, top researchers estimate that genetics are responsible for 60 to 90 percent of cases.[8] How could the number of kids with a condition that is predominantly genetic double within a single generation? One plausible explanation is that roughly the same percentage of children and adults experience the same biologically based propensity to struggle when asked to sustain attention to uninteresting tasks, organize and complete tasks, prioritize tasks, manage time, delay gratification, self-regulate emotions, and modulate impulses today as compared with thirty years ago, but the challenges of daily life for someone with traits associated with ADHD are far more serious today. For some kids with ADHD, fulfilling the academic demands of high school is akin to expecting the goldfish in the cartoon to climb a tree.

We know that one in nine school-age children in the United States have been prescribed medication for ADHD and that most cases are attributable to genetics. Yet the research indicates that only 4 percent of adults are diagnosed with ADHD.[9] And while available research suggests that some people "outgrow" select features of ADHD (impulsivity and hyperactivity) as brain maturation continues into the early twenties, brain maturation alone doesn't account for such a pronounced drop in ADHD rates between the teen years and adulthood. Something else is going on here.

I believe one factor in this difference is the fact that adults are free to choose the environments in which they spend most of their time—their career, specific workplace, home, and recreation. I've observed that a significant number of teens with ADHD can discontinue or greatly reduce their use of prescription medication when they go to college while achieving academic success, because they are free to select a major in an area of study they experience as interesting or directly relevant to their career aspirations. When teens and young adults treated for ADHD complete school, they often seek jobs in which the functional demands are a good fit with the way their brain processes information. Anecdotally, many parents of my patients with ADHD who themselves were treated for ADHD in their youth become entrepreneurs. They tend to be visionaries who don't like other people telling them what to do. If they're smart enough to hire managers with good organizational skills to make up for their struggle in attending to details, their business ventures are often very successful. Some seek out jobs that require lots of travel because they struggle with boredom when working in the same office with the same people, day in and day out. Many excel in sales positions because bonuses and financial incentives provide added motivation. The key point is that many are no longer "disabled" in that their genetically based condition no longer interferes with major life activities.

Your church will be ready to embrace the potential influx of gifts and talents from new attendees drawn to your church if its leadership is debating and discerning the value of launching a deliberate mental health inclusion initiative.

Paul reminds us in 1 Corinthians that Christ didn't decide to build his church by putting together an all-star team of believers who had achieved great success through overcoming the challenges presented in the culture:

> Brothers and sisters, think of what you were when you were called. Not many of you were wise by human standards; not many were influential; not many were of noble birth. But God chose the foolish things of the world to shame the wise; God chose the weak things of the world to shame the strong. God chose the lowly things of this world and the despised things—and the things that are not—to nullify the things that are, so that no one may boast before him.
>
> *1 Corinthians 1:26–29*

DOES THE CULTURE OF THE CHURCH CAUSE DISABILITY?

Ben Conner is a theology professor and disability advocate who has written of his experience leading groups for teens and young adults with autism. Ben's observations on the nature of disability are a great starting place for understanding how our expectations for the way people should act, think, communicate, and relate at church present challenges for children and adults with common mental health conditions and for their families:

> It is our culture that disables . . . When one is dis-abled, the problem is not really that they have impairments and social skill deficits. The issue at stake is that they live in an "ableist" culture that rarely affords them the space or opportunity to make their unique contribution to society and does not lift up the value of choosing them as friends.[10]

Ben reminds us of our propensity to devalue people who don't readily meet our expectations or fit easily into the majority culture. We're quick to focus on what people can't do while overlooking the God-given gifts and talents everyone has been given to contribute to the fulfillment of the church's mission in the world.

Men, women, and children with all types of disability all too often experience the feeling of being outsiders in the culture and sense there is no place for them to contribute and belong. Fifteen years of serving in the disability ministry movement and thirty years of caring for children and families affected by mental illness have led me to conclude that they're no more likely—and may even be less likely—to experience that sense of belonging at church compared to other places in our culture.

Church leaders and attendees need to consider the ways in which the culture within our churches—customs and practices for gathering together for worship and the environments we create for ministry—perpetuate disability. Features of a broad range of common mental health conditions make it harder for people with those conditions to participate in our customs, practices, and ministry environments. Our willingness to examine ways that we can make our church gatherings more welcoming to people with disabilities—including those with mental health disabilities—is a good barometer of the extent to which we value them and recognize them as fellow image bearers of God.

How do we make our churches more welcoming? Consider the steps we often take when we anticipate house guests to ensure they'll feel safe and comfortable during their visit. Most people would go to the trouble of childproofing their electrical outlets if they know a toddler is coming to visit. A good host will ensure they have food to eat for a guest with dietary restrictions. You probably wouldn't invite someone with asthma or another respiratory condition for a drive and then proceed to smoke in the car. We'll explore many ideas for extending hospitality to our church guests with common mental health conditions in the second part of this book.

▪ ▪ ▪

Let me share a story from my practice to illustrate how the culture of a church might influence the experience of a family when a child has a significant mental health condition.

A young couple came to our office with their six-year-old son, Henry. They were referred by the special education department of their son's school. When I asked Henry's parents to share the single biggest concern that brought them to my office, they described their family's inability to pursue any of the fun activities their neighbors enjoyed—things like movies, vacations, amusement parks, and camping trips—because Henry's lack of self-control greatly limited their ability to go out in public as a family.

When I evaluate new patients, I usually conduct both a lengthy interview with the child in the absence of their parents and an interview with the parents while the child entertains himself or herself in another room. During my interview with Henry, he was *literally* bouncing off the furniture and walls in my office. When I was meeting with Henry's parents, I reviewed their questionnaire, which we ask all new families to complete, and I noted—with great surprise—that the only activity the family did together was *go to church*. I couldn't imagine how this kid was able to hold it together at church. The reports I reviewed from Henry's school, in combination with his parents' accounts of his behavior outside the home and my own personal experience with him in my office, suggested that he lacked the self-control to meet the expectations for behavior at a church service. I was curious. I asked Henry's parents how they attended church when they couldn't do anything else in public as a family.

They said, "We sit in the first row. There's lots of room between the front row and the stage. He and his brother like to dance to the praise band. When the music is over, they take the kids out and keep them busy. He does OK." Henry thrived at his church, despite severe self-control problems associated with ADHD, because the church's worship style, behavioral expectations, and design of their children's ministry programming were a good fit for him. Had his parents tried attending another church in our area that had more defined expectations for how children should behave at worship services or a more traditional worship style, Henry and his family probably wouldn't have lasted more than fifteen minutes.

I don't mean to suggest that churches must adopt contemporary worship music or hold services in a renovated movie theatre if they hope to welcome families of kids who have ADHD or other mental health challenges. I have kids who come into my practice with autism spectrum disorders, accompanied by significant sensory processing issues, and they would probably run out the back door of Henry's church when the loud music and dancing began at the beginning of the service. If they were to make it through the music with the assistance of their noise-canceling headphones, the light show would undoubtedly be their undoing.

There is no single church for everyone. Keep that in mind as you contemplate how your church might welcome and include families with disabilities, including those who have mental health disabilities. Your church will never be able to create a culture that will be perfect for *every* child or *every* adult with *every* conceivable disability. But *every* church can do *something* to welcome more families impacted by disability—including mental illness. I'll talk about what "doing more" looks like in later chapters.

■ ■ ■

Let me conclude our discussion on the nature of mental health-related disability and church by introducing you to another family I worked with.

I first met Lisa and her parents when she was underachieving academically in elementary school. Her school had speculated that her lack of academic progress was caused by poor attention, focus, and self-control. The team at school had noted that she struggled to make and keep friends. During her school's evaluation to determine Lisa's eligibility for special education services, she was identified with social (pragmatic) communication disorder (SCD). In Lisa's case, this condition manifested in an inability to intuitively grasp the right words to say or right actions to take in unstructured or unfamiliar social situations. Lisa also complained with increasing frequency of a broad array of physical complaints (headaches, stomach aches, chest discomfort). Her physical complaints coincided with periods of heightened anxiety and resulted in increasingly frequent absences from school.

I had diagnosed Lisa with separation anxiety disorder and ADHD, in addition to the social pragmatic language disorder identified by her team at school. Lisa and her family met regularly with a counselor to give her techniques for managing her anxiety and provide her parents with strategies to employ when her anxiety resulted in daily battles over leaving for school. Medication prescribed for ADHD was discontinued because the benefits were minimal, and Lisa experienced heightened anxiety as a side effect. Medication for anxiety worsened her challenges with self-control.

Her parents had the means to enroll her in a private school that offered innovative educational approaches for kids with attention and learning differences. She quickly began to thrive academically, but her anxiety symptoms worsened as the school day progressed. Before the transfer, she had lived in close physical proximity to her public school— close enough that she could see it from her bedroom window. Her new school was a thirty-minute one-way drive from her home, intensifying her irrational fears that she or her mother would be harmed during the time they were separated for school. Lisa and her mother made good use of the counseling services they were offered, and her separation fears gradually resolved over several months. We didn't see or hear from them for several years. Her grades were good, and she made—and kept—new friends. Her new environment at school was a good fit.

Several years later, I received a call from Lisa's mom asking for our help on an emergency basis. Lisa had become extremely angry during an argument at home and repeatedly punched and kicked her mother. Her mother was in the process of calling the police when a relative paid an unexpected visit and succeeded in separating the two of them.

The argument had started when Lisa's mother insisted she attend the overnight retreat sponsored by their church's middle school ministry.

While sorting out the situation, I learned that Lisa attended church every week but always sat with her parents in the adult worship service. She almost never attended the middle school worship service offered at the same time as the adult service in a separate auditorium on the other end of her church's campus. Upon further questioning, I learned that Lisa got along well with the seven other kids in her class at her alternative school and continued to perform well academically, but she had declined every sleepover invitation received from classmates since transferring to the alternative school three years earlier. She didn't appear to experience anxiety at her athletic practices or events because her mother provided transportation to her events and accompanied her to all extracurricular activities.

Lisa's meltdown with her mother over the middle school church retreat was a manifestation of her underlying anxiety. She had overcome her challenges with social communication within her small and familiar peer group, but she continued to experience anxiety at the prospect of interacting with unfamiliar kids from outside her specialized school. The thought of the middle school retreat triggered a recurrence of her separation anxiety. She faced the challenge of spending an entire weekend apart from her parents with a large group of kids whom she didn't know on an island in the middle of Lake Erie that was accessible only by ferries that operated during the day.

Her parents pushed her to attend the retreat because of the social pressure they received from the middle school pastor, who had called or texted them several times a week in the month leading up to the retreat. Her parents were worried about what this pastor and other parents in the church might think if word got out about Lisa's struggles with anxiety, and they hoped the occasional questions about their daughter's absence from middle school ministry programming would go away if she attended the retreat.

Let's consider how Lisa's situation reflects the unique attributes of mental health disability.

- Lisa's difficulties with inattention, lack of focus, and poor self-control that led to her ADHD diagnosis were no longer disabling in her alternative school setting.

- Lisa's childhood has been characterized by episodes of heightened anxiety that last for weeks or months with extended periods during which she has minimal symptoms—an inability to accept sleepover invitations, for example. Her most recent anxiety episode resulted in major challenges at home and church but had little impact on her success at school.

- Lisa's parents were reluctant to disclose the reasons for her absence from middle school ministry activities despite attending a church well-known throughout the area for its special needs ministry.

- The leaders of Lisa's church likely had no idea why she was sitting in the sanctuary with her parents every Sunday, and they never learned why she didn't show up at the middle school retreat or what her family endured when they tried to make her attend. But Lisa and her family are fortunate. *They still go to church.*

Fifty million children and adults in the United States have a diagnosed mental health condition. Mental illness is the leading cause of disability both in the United States and worldwide. Whether we realize it or not, our expectations at church for social interaction and conduct, when combined with the physical properties and functional demands of our ministry environments, represent significant barriers to church involvement for children and adults with common mental health conditions and for their families. Church can feel like *hostile territory* for families impacted by mental illness.

In the next two chapters, I'll identify seven common barriers to church involvement for children and adults with mental health conditions.

THREE

The First Two Barriers to Church Involvement

Americans who never attend church services are the least likely to agree that churches welcome those with mental illness. Those who attend weekly see churches as welcoming.

LIFEWAY RESEARCH, 2013 SURVEY

In the last chapter, we were introduced to Lisa—the girl from our practice whose aggressive behavior was triggered by her parents' insistence that she attend a weekend middle school ministry retreat. We observed how she became overwhelmed by the prospect of a weekend church retreat on an island in the middle of Lake Erie during which she would need to interact with dozens of kids she didn't know well.

It turns out there are lots of children and adults like Lisa with a wide array of mental health conditions for whom the prospect of attending church causes great trepidation.

LifeWay Research's 2013 study reported that more than half (55 percent) of US adults surveyed who don't currently attend worship services *disagreed* with this statement: "If I had a mental health issue, I believe most churches would welcome me."[1] More than half of the adults surveyed who don't attend worship services believe the American church is not a safe or welcoming place for persons with mental illness. At the very least, the church has an image problem among outsiders with regard to our attitudes about mental health.

The LifeWay study also pointed to an enormous disconnect between perceptions of church insiders (those who regularly attend worship services at least once a week) and those outside the church over the receptiveness of churches to persons with mental illness. A large percentage (79 percent) of regular church attenders surveyed by LifeWay endorsed their churches as welcoming places. Unfortunately, the study investigators failed to ask appropriate follow-up questions to identify *why* outsiders view the church as inhospitable.

In my conversations over the last twenty-five years with families served by our practice, I've learned that many had been regular church attenders who left following a negative personal experience—either something they experienced themselves or an episode involving their child. The stories they share with friends, neighbors, and colleagues influence perceptions of the church's receptiveness to persons with mental illness.

I suspect the wide divergence in the expectations and beliefs about mental illness held by Christians from more conservative theological traditions compared to those endorsed by the general population as reported in the LifeWay study also contributes to the public image of the church regarding mental illness. Of those who identify themselves as born-again evangelical or fundamentalist Christians, 48 percent endorsed the statement that people with serious mental illnesses like depression, bipolar disorder, and schizophrenia can overcome their conditions *through Bible study and prayer alone.* Only 27 percent of other Americans agree.[2]

I believe most pastors and church leaders are unaware of the extent to which the experience of a mental health disorder—"serious" mental health conditions such as depression, bipolar disorder, or schizophrenia *and* more common conditions, including anxiety disorders, ADHD, and PTSD—impacts attendance and engagement in worship services and church programming. Most have likely given little thought to how someone with social skill deficits can fit into a church where small group participation is expected, how a first-time visitor with social anxiety might experience a worship service in which newcomers are singled out for special recognition, or how the bustle and chaos of the children's ministry check-in process might affect the family of a child who has sensory processing differences.

Churches represent subcultures with norms and expectations—often unwritten—for appropriate conduct and social interaction. Let's consider the behavioral expectations for kids attending children's ministry programming. We expect school-age children to listen quietly when adults are talking, to follow directions the first time, to raise their hand and ask permission before speaking, to take turns speaking (and allow others to speak without interruption), to keep their hands and feet to themselves, to demonstrate respect to teachers and one another, to maintain high levels of self-control, and to suppress any aggressive impulses toward peers or adults.

Furthermore, we assume that when kids come to church, they will easily separate from their parents or caregivers upon arrival and tolerate separation from parents or caregivers during the worship service. We assume children will be comfortable interacting with unfamiliar peers, speaking when they're spoken to, and reading aloud in front of a group. Kids with common mental health conditions often struggle to meet those expectations.

An essential first step for church leaders who want to minister more effectively with individuals and families affected by mental illness is to acknowledge that assumptions regarding the ability of attendees and visitors to meet our expectations for conduct or social interaction may need to be revisited. A next step involves developing a deeper understanding of how children and adults with common mental health conditions experience our ministry environments differently than other attendees do. Church leaders involved in inclusion efforts can then review established ministry customs and practices from the perspective of a child, teen, or adult affected by a significant condition.

In the remainder of this chapter and in the following chapter, I'll introduce you to seven ways in which the experience of having a mental illness can represent a barrier to church attendance or participation. The first four of these barriers represent specific traits or attributes associated with common mental conditions—or with an array of mental health conditions. They are stigma, anxiety, executive functioning, and sensory processing. I'll cover the first two—stigma and anxiety—in this chapter. These are among the most common barriers that families and individuals face when trying to participate in the life of a church. In the next chapter, I'll look at the final five barriers.

THE FIRST BARRIER: STIGMA

In the previous chapter, I identified several attributes of mental illness that require a different approach to ministry than the strategies currently used for persons with *special needs*—physical, intellectual, and developmental disabilities. One of the attributes was the *hidden* nature of mental illness—our inability to know from looking at someone whether they have a disability and if our words and actions are likely to be helpful or hurtful. Our challenge in serving those with mental illness is heightened because they often try hard to hide their disability from others. They may be especially hesitant to share psychiatric diagnoses they've been given by mental health or medical professionals or discuss past or current treatments.

I often find the children and families served by my practice to be very reluctant to disclose the presence of a mental health condition to teachers, school administrators, coaches, and other adults involved in the child's life—including grandparents or extended family members. Many refuse to accept beneficial accommodations and supports. *Stigma* perpetuates the resistance to acknowledge the presence of a mental health condition and to seek effective treatment. We need to recognize how two different types of stigma impact the challenges churches face in outreach to individuals and families impacted by mental illness—the *stigma in our general culture* connected to persons with mental illness and specific treatments for mental illness, and the *stigma uniquely connected with mental illness in the church*. Let's examine how each type of stigma impacts our efforts to welcome children and adults into our churches.

More than half of the patients in my practice are teens. During their years in middle school and high school, they experience significant pressure from their peers to conform to interests, fashion, and behavior common to their subculture. Most kids in my practice are terrified by the prospect of being viewed as "different" by their peers. They may resist accepting any help that could lead to undesired attention from their peers.

My practice serves an area known for its outstanding public school systems. Families of children with special education needs often purchase homes within specific school districts because of the availability of excellent support services. Nevertheless, many kids in my practice with identified support needs who are offered services by their schools don't receive them. If I were making a conservative estimate, I would say that up to half of my patients who qualify for school-based accommodations or special education services *refuse* the support they need. Why do they refuse help? Many tell me they're embarrassed to be seen walking into a special education classroom or dread feeling pressured to explain to their friends why they get extra time for tests or take tests in a different room than the rest of their class does.

This observation points to why most children and teens with common mental health conditions are poorly served by the special needs ministries established in recent years by a growing number of churches. As we'll note later, a broad array of mental health conditions has been associated with challenges in emotional regulation, social communication, and self-control. Over time, they often internalize a sense of being "different" from others. Subtle differences in thinking, speech, and behavior from their peers make them prime targets for bullying. The resulting hurt and shame often produce a determination to avoid the attention of others. Many of the kids I've come to know through our practice desperately seek to blend in to what others are doing while avoiding the notice of their peers.

The takeaway for pastors and church leaders is that kids with mental health-related disabilities and their families will flee from any ministry programming or activities that draw attention to their differences. Attempts to serve them through a ministry designed for persons with obvious physical, intellectual, or developmental disabilities will intensify their sense of being different from their peers and are likely doomed to failure.

Many children and teens don't get the support they need at church because their parents are unaware that their child has a problem. I often ask parents who come to our practice after years of family conflict, academic underachievement, and difficulties with peers why they waited so long to seek help. A frequent response reflects the attitudes and beliefs associated with mental illness in our culture: "I didn't want my child to be labeled." When parents avoid seeking professional help because of fear their kids will be stigmatized, their children lose the potential benefits of simple, nonintrusive accommodations or strategies that can enhance their experiences of school, home, extracurricular activities, *and church*. The parent who remains unaware of their child's social anxiety or performance anxiety may fail to recognize that the meltdowns they witness when they tell their child to get ready for church may stem from their child's fear of being called on to answer questions or to read aloud from the Bible in front of a large group of peers at Sunday school.

I'll share another illustration of the stigma associated with mental health treatment. When my practice first opened, our office space was located on the second floor of a two-story bank building prominently situated at one of our county's busiest intersections. The building sits in front of a busy grocery store. Many of our appointments are scheduled at times when kids are out of school—late afternoons, early evenings, or Saturday afternoons—all of which are times when banks are closed. A part-time counselor from our practice described how her daily routine led her to drive past our office at different times throughout the day. She observed that families with scheduled appointments would routinely park their cars in the grocery store lot and sneak across the grass that separated the two lots with their children, *especially* when the bank was closed. The inconvenience of trekking across the wet (and often snow-covered) grass was less of a concern to image-conscious parents than their neighbors' speculation as to why their car was parked at our office. When our office moved, I selected a building that already housed several pediatric dental practices and an orthodontist, so our families could be less self-conscious in coming to our office.

Is it any wonder that parents who resist sharing information about their child's mental health diagnosis or treatment with the teachers and counselors who spend much of the day with them or are embarrassed to be seen near a psychiatrist's office are unlikely to disclose their child's emotional or behavioral challenges to church staff or volunteers? Is anyone surprised when a man or woman who suddenly stops coming to a church or a Bible study they've attended for years chooses not to tell anyone that fatigue associated with their depression keeps them bedridden for weeks at a time?

▪ ▪ ▪

I began this chapter with study findings describing the common perception among outsiders that the church is unwelcoming to persons with mental illness. What if their perceptions are true? Is there a reason to believe that *mental health stigma is worse in the church* than in the broader society? Let's examine the origins of beliefs and perceptions regarding mental illness that persist in large segments of the North American church. We'll begin with Sigmund Freud.

Freud was a prominent physician who developed the theory of psychoanalysis to treat patients with unexplained neurologic symptoms. His theoretical framework viewed guilt as pathological and rejected the idea that guilt is a warning from the conscience of the need to recognize and deal with sin. The psychodynamic psychotherapies derived from Freud's work attribute behavior to instinctive urges or drives—a stark contrast to centuries of Christian teaching that view human behavior as actions that result from man's exercise of his God-given freedom to choose right from wrong, for which the individual bears personal responsibility.

Freud's attempts to understand human nature through observation and the scientific method served as a catalyst to the development of behaviorism. Behaviorism's two foundational assumptions are that (1) nature is the only reality, and (2) reality can only be measured through our senses. From a Christian perspective, behaviorism is fatally flawed because its practitioners fail to consider the spiritual dimensions of human existence that can't be readily quantified and measured. Pure behaviorism is antithetical to the construct of free will and the biblical teaching on the importance of the soul.

Humanistic therapies emerged in response to the determinism inherent in psychoanalytic and behavioral theory. The goal of humanistic therapies is self-fulfillment and self-actualization. Therapy is conducted with the assumption that the individual is responsible for their own happiness and accountable to only themselves. The emphasis in humanism on subjective experience and rejection of moral absolutes is incompatible with two thousand years of Christian teaching. Adherents of humanism struggle to acknowledge there's a God to whom man is accountable.

Albert Ellis was the developer of rational emotive therapy in the mid-1950s and a major intellectual force behind the advance of moral relativism.[3] Ellis was arguably the most influential psychologist of the 1960s. Ellis's growing cultural influence triggered a movement among professors from theologically conservative seminaries that viewed psychiatry and psychology as dangerous forces. Many influential pastors and church leaders concluded it was impossible for Christians to be helped by therapies grounded in understandings of humanity incompatible with long-held biblical truths. Psychotherapy constituted a threat to the faith of believers.

If Sigmund Freud had an outsized role in the growth of modern psychiatry, Jay Adams had a similarly outsized role in the growth of the biblical counseling movement. For the past fifty years, Adams has helped shape understanding of mental illness among pastors and church leaders within evangelical and Reformed traditions. Now in his late eighties, Adams continues to teach and write, although his influence has diminished in recent decades.

What was so revolutionary about Adams and his view of psychiatry and psychology? In his landmark book *Competent to Counsel* (first published in 1970), Adams presented a construct that continues to carry great influence in the church.[4] He rejected the modern concept of mental illness:

> To put the issue simply: the Scriptures plainly speak of both organically based problems as well as those problems that stem from sinful action and behavior; but where, in all of God's Word, is there so much as a trace of any third source of problems which might approximate the modern concept of "mental illness"?[5]

Adams was very blunt in his assessment of persons with mental illness and the treatment provided by mental health professionals.

> What, then, is wrong with the "mentally ill"? Their problem is autogenic; it is in themselves. The fundamental bent of human nature is away from God. Man is born in sin, goes astray "from his mother's womb speaking lies" (Psalm 58:3) and will therefore naturally (by nature) attempt various sinful dodges in an attempt to avoid facing up to his sin. He will fall into varying styles of sin according to the short-term successes or failures of the particular sinful responses which he makes to life's problems. Apart from organically generated difficulties, the mentally ill are really *people with unsolved personal problems.*[6]

Adams continues to voice strong opinions about where Christians with emotional or behavioral concerns should turn for help. In *The Christian Counselor's Manual*, he wrote:

> Biblically, there is no warrant for acknowledging the existence of a separate and distinct discipline called psychiatry. There are, in the Scriptures, only three specified sources of personal problems in living: demonic activity (principally possession), personal sin, and organic illness. These three are interrelated. All options are covered under these heads, leaving no room for a fourth: non-organic mental illness. There is, therefore, no place in a biblical scheme for the psychiatrist as a separate practitioner.[7]

To summarize the essentials of the teaching of Jay Adams, everything we need to counsel people for emotional or behavioral problems that aren't *unequivocally* organic can be found in Scripture. The Bible is sufficient for counseling. The underlying cause of mental illness is sin. Mental health practitioners dissuade people from taking responsibility for their emotions and behavior.

Adams also wrote extensively of the importance of grace in the counseling process. Unfortunately, many pastors and biblical counselors embraced the "sin" and "truth" components of Adams's model and forgot about the "grace" he emphasized. Too many Christians share stories of pain and hurt resulting from their experiences in seeking help from their churches for mental health conditions. A woman named Kristin shared her family's experience in response to a Key Ministry blog post:

> Twenty years ago, I was repeatedly told by many people that I just needed to pray harder and that if my relationship with Jesus was better, my severe depression would be healed ... But my depression was not healed. I left the church for several years, but returned hoping that not all Christians thought that way. Of course, I also didn't tell too many church friends about my mental illness.

Fast-forward to the present. I now have two children with severe mental illness. Last year, my daughter was forced to join a Sunday school class in which she knew no other child. I tried in vain to explain that she had severe social anxiety and needed to be in a class where she had a friend. Because of that, she wasn't happy in Sunday school and ended up quitting the children's choir too. We hardly ever go to church any more. I write this with tears in my eyes because I want to find a church where my kids and I are accepted, and yes, even given "special" treatment from time to time.[8]

Prominent and influential church leaders openly disparage the use of medication for treatment of mental health conditions in terms that would be unthinkable for other medical treatments. John MacArthur is the founder of The Master's Seminary in Southern California and a respected pastor and Bible teacher featured on the popular radio broadcast *Grace to You*. MacArthur preached a sermon as part of a series titled "God's Pattern for Children" that would cause any parent in attendance to think twice before coming to church with a child lacking self-control.

It takes a lot of time to train a child, a lot less time to give him a pill. But turning your disobedient child, your child that lacks self-control, maybe your angry child because that child is not cared for properly, turning that child into a drug addict, is that a solution? . . .

Every kid is like that if he's not taught self-control . . .

I had a lot going on in my head, and I couldn't concentrate on just one thing because I was busy with a whole lot of things . . . I'm glad my parents didn't turn me into a drug addict. I didn't have a disease or a disorder, that was just me.[9]

I've had many parents ask my opinion of statements and teachings offered at church along the line of Dr. MacArthur's. I often find myself biting my tongue. I don't know if the family is quoting their pastor accurately or taking their statements out of context. Dr. MacArthur is a fabulous Bible teacher. Two heavily highlighted copies of his study Bible sit in my study. But I become very frustrated when church leaders commit too many "unforced errors," to borrow a tennis expression. If our mission as the church is to "go and make disciples," I don't see how shaming parents of kids with serious emotional or behavior conditions who comply with treatment recommendations offered by trained professionals helps to enhance their receptiveness to the gospel.

Put yourself in the shoes of a parent of a child who has a serious behavior problem. If you and your spouse are still married to one another, your relationship is likely to be strained. You're likely exhausted from the time and energy you've been spending responding to your child's provocations. You may be experiencing financial difficulties resulting from the cost of your child's treatments. If your child is taking medication, you probably thought long and hard before agreeing to the medication. How would you react if you came to church seeking truth, encouragement, and hope only to hear that your child's behavior problems result from your insufficient care and that the medication you agreed to reluctantly, at the urging of your child's physician, will cause your child long-term harm? Would you come back?

What if you *don't* have a child who has problem behaviors but you hear a message like that at church? How likely are you to invite a friend, neighbor, or coworker to church if you know their child has issues with self-control? Not very likely, I'd guess.

Pastors don't bear all the responsibility for the church's reputation for being less than welcoming to families impacted by mental illness. John Rosemond is a popular speaker and author who has a syndicated newspaper column. Links to his interviews and webcasts are featured on websites extending support to Christian families. In Rosemond's book, *The Diseasing of America's Children*, he writes:

> But is ADHD a "disorder"? Does its nomenclature accurately reflect that there is something amiss with the children in

question, that for whatever reason—biological or otherwise—
they can't "think straight," and thus their behavior is often
chaotically disorganized? Or is attention-deficit/hyperactivity
disorder simply a more scientific-sounding way of referring to
what, not so long ago, people simply called a spoiled brat?[10]

Now imagine yourself as a parent of a child with ADHD who attends
a church that is hosting one of Rosemond's parenting seminars. Would you
tell anyone in the children's ministry department about your child's need
for additional support? Would you speak freely in a small group about the
day-to-day parenting challenges you experience? Would you feel comfortable
asking others at church to pray for you and your family? Or would shame
or guilt lead you to hide that part of your life from others at church?

We're too quick in the church to conceptualize mental illness as an
either-or choice between science and the Bible or between medical and
spiritual solutions and do damage to families in the process. There are
times when mental health problems *are* a consequence of sin. It's not
unusual for me to see kids experience signs of anxiety or depression or
to report the presence of suicidal thoughts after making the choice to
become sexually active. Lots of children's struggles with self-control
result from the effects of stress hormones on brain development following parental neglect or trauma. I don't presume to know the cause of a
child's problems without taking the time to get to know the child and
their family. Neither should pastors and other church leaders.

THE SECOND BARRIER: ANXIETY

Imagine having an untreated medical condition that causes your brain
to flood your bloodstream with stress hormones when you find yourself surrounded by unfamiliar people in unfamiliar settings. What
symptoms might you experience? Among them may be headaches,
chest pain, nausea, heartburn, dizziness, diarrhea, muscle weakness,
and difficulty breathing. Your physical distress may be accompanied by

an overwhelming sense of dread and thoughts of getting to a hospital as quickly as possible. You would likely go to great lengths to avoid entering the types of situations that trigger your condition.

How difficult would it be for you to persuade a friend, neighbor, or coworker with a similar condition to visit your church for the first time? And what's the likelihood of them coming back to your church if they get sick on their initial visit?

Let's explore why many children and adults with common anxiety disorders avoid worship services and church activities.

What Causes Anxiety Disorders?

The dictionary defines *anxiety* as "a painful or apprehensive uneasiness of mind usually over an impending or anticipated ill" or as "an abnormal and overwhelming sense of apprehension and fear often marked by physiological signs (as sweating, tension, and increased pulse), by doubt concerning the reality and nature of the threat, and by self-doubt about one's capacity to cope with it." Anxiety is a normal and healthy response to *future* threats, while fear describes the emotional response to *imminent* threat, whether real or perceived. Someone with an identified *anxiety disorder* experiences excessive and persistent anxiety or fear inappropriate for their level of maturity that significantly interferes with tasks of daily living.

Multiple factors contribute to one's risk of developing an anxiety disorder—or offer protection from anxiety. They include:

- *Genetic predisposition.* Small contributions from many genes are thought to represent 30 to 40 percent of the variability in anxiety rates.
- *Temperament.* This refers to the qualities of an individual's personality that are innate as opposed to learned. Children with a shy temperament are at greater risk for anxiety disorders.
- *Brain circuitry.* Neuroimaging studies have demonstrated a relationship between abnormal limbic system activity (the brain

area responsible for modulating emotions) and the propensity for overestimating risk. Abnormal connections between the limbic system and the prefrontal cortex (an area of the brain responsible for higher order thinking and self-control) have been associated with anxiety disorders.

- *Brain chemistry.* At least six different neurotransmitters (chemicals responsible for transmitting electrical impulses from one cell to another in the nervous system) have been shown to contribute to anxiety symptoms. Medications typically work by increasing or decreasing the activity of one or two neurotransmitters.

- *Learned behavior.* Parents often model inappropriate responses to anxiety-provoking situations for their children and unintentionally reinforce maladaptive coping strategies and patterns of avoidance.

- *Trauma.* Children who have experienced trauma, neglect, abuse, and other adverse childhood experiences are at greater risk of developing anxiety disorders.

- *Medical conditions.* Thyroid disease, asthma, chronic obstructive pulmonary disease (COPD), heart disease, diabetes, chronic pain, and irritable bowel syndrome have been shown to cause anxiety symptoms.

- *Medications.* Prescription medications (and readily available over-the-counter medications) often produce or exacerbate anxiety. A common cause of anxiety symptoms among patients referred to my practice is stimulant medication prescribed for ADHD. Sudden discontinuation of anti-anxiety medication often results in heightened anxiety along with withdrawal symptoms.

Let's consider two additional sources of anxiety. *Anxiety may result from a propensity to misinterpret information.* Children and adults with anxiety disorders often hold wildly inaccurate perceptions—some conscious, some unconscious—of the impressions they make on others. For example, you spot someone at the mall you think you know from high school. Instead of approaching them to say hello, you duck into the first store you can find and pretend to shop, because the first thought that popped into your mind when you spotted them was that they won't remember you and you will have made a fool of yourself. These irrational assumptions often cause those with anxiety disorders to deliberately avoid pleasurable activities and relationships. The most common evidence-based treatment for children and adults with anxiety disorders—cognitive-behavioral therapy (CBT)—is predicated in part on identifying and managing thinking errors that contribute to emotional and physical distress.

We experience anxiety because of the choices we make. I know firsthand how choices affect our lives. My procrastination in high school—when I needed to be studying for chemistry or calculus tests, for example—frequently resulted in intense anxiety. Kids who give in to the urge to stick their hands in the cookie jar and adults who do things they know they shouldn't do may experience anxiety because they know they are being disobedient and worry about getting caught. As we saw in our exploration of stigma, we *sometimes* experience anxiety because of sin.

Medical and mental health professionals use a diagnostic classification system to describe common patterns of anxiety organized around either the nature of their symptoms or the situations in which they experience functional impairment. Persons with anxiety may experience symptoms of more than one anxiety disorder, and over time, a person predisposed to anxiety may meet the criteria for different anxiety disorders at different times in life. I've found that each anxiety disorder is often associated with specific challenges to church involvement.

Children and teens with *separation anxiety disorder* typically experience excessive fear or distress when away from home or significant attachment figures, usually parents. Church activities in which children and parents are served in different physical locations where they can't see one another may result in heightened anxiety, manifested by tearfulness, anger, or irritability. Retreats and mission trips involving one or more nights away from home often cause intense anxiety for older children and teens unless they're accompanied by a parent.

Children or adults with a *specific phobia* experience fear of certain objects or situations. Their fear in the presence of the object or situation often leads to the development of elaborate avoidance strategies. Someone with a fear of germs may avoid shaking hands with members of the welcome team positioned at church entrances or dread the prospect of greeting fellow worshipers at the direction of the pastor during a service. A fear of flying may be a more plausible explanation than a lack of faithfulness for someone's reluctance to participate in an overseas mission trip. Someone with a fear of flames may avoid volunteering at candlelight services.

Children and adults with *social anxiety disorder* experience significant fear and distress in situations where their words or actions may be exposed to the scrutiny of others. The person often fears they will act in a way that will result in embarrassment or humiliation. A first-time visitor to church may be preoccupied by concerns that they are being judged on the basis of their words or personal appearance. They may avoid church entirely because of horror stories of newcomers being handed a microphone to speak or being introduced to the entire congregation in the middle of a worship service.

Children and adults with *panic disorder* experience brief, recurrent, unanticipated episodes of intense fear, accompanied by a characteristic set of physical symptoms, a sense of impending doom, and the urge to flee the place where they experience symptoms. *Agoraphobia* is a closely related condition in which intense symptoms of anxiety occur in situations experienced as unsafe with no easy way to escape—often experienced in cars, trains, planes, elevators, and tunnels. The absence of an aisle seat at church located near an exit to facilitate an unobtrusive escape may be sufficient to trigger an attack for someone with agoraphobia.

Children and adults with *obsessive-compulsive disorder* (OCD) experience recurrent, intrusive thoughts or compulsive, recurrent, repetitive behaviors associated with significant mental distress. They may struggle with excessive perfectionism or with making and sticking to decisions, or they may fear they will be compelled to perform certain actions against their will. They may develop time-consuming rituals for counting, checking, arranging, or ordering items; grooming; or washing. Someone with OCD who also has contamination fears may go to great lengths to avoid physical contact with other worshipers or with objects or furniture at church that have been contaminated. Children and teens with OCD in our practice who come from Christian families are especially prone to episodes of intense anxiety if they begin questioning their salvation, developing obsessive fears of acting violently toward loved ones, or engaging in sexual behavior against their will.

Full participation in the church often requires vulnerability, social risk, and change—all of which can be incredibly challenging for those with anxiety. We as church leaders can demonstrate Christ's love for persons who struggle with anxiety by graciously helping them join our ministry environments and providing them with the necessary supports that will allow them to grow alongside the rest of the church.

■　■　■

Stigma and anxiety represent two of the most common barriers that people with mental health conditions face when considering participation in the church. But they are not the only barriers. In the next chapter, I'll consider five additional barriers that families and individuals face, beginning with a diminished capacity to exercise self-restraint and self-discipline associated with a wide range of mental health disorders.

---| FOUR |---

Five Additional Barriers

In the last chapter, we looked at the first two barriers that keep people with mental health conditions from full participation in the life of a local church—stigma and anxiety. These represent *specific traits or attributes* associated with mental health conditions, as do the first two barriers in this chapter: executive functioning and sensory processing. The remaining three barriers represent *social consequences* resulting from the experience of mental illness.

Let's begin by looking at how executive functioning represents a barrier to church involvement for many persons with mental illness.

THE THIRD BARRIER: EXECUTIVE FUNCTIONING

Those immersed in church culture recognize that a well-developed capacity for self-discipline is considered a sign of spiritual maturity. Conversely, the inability to control one's words and actions is taken to reflect spiritual immaturity. One attribute associated with significant functional impairment in persons with common (ADHD, anxiety disorders) and serious (schizophrenia, bipolar disorder, major depression, disruptive mood dysregulation) mental health conditions is diminished executive functioning.

Medical and mental health professionals use the term *executive functioning* to refer to the set of cognitive abilities involved in modulating other abilities and behaviors. Executive functions represent the means through which we develop language, plan for our future, set priorities, manage time, delay gratification, and exercise conscious control over our thoughts, words, and actions. Our executive functions are highly interdependent on one another. In accordance with our human nature as described in Scripture (see Romans 3:9–20), our executive functioning capacity is imperfect. No one can fulfill the requirements of God's law or provide sufficient atonement for their sins. We all need Jesus! Yet we are often quick to judge our brothers and sisters who experience greater struggle in hiding their imperfections from others in the church.

We'll examine briefly how weaknesses in key executive functions may contribute to challenges with church attendance and participation.[1] The five categories of executive functions we'll discuss in this section are:

- behavioral inhibition
- verbal working memory
- nonverbal working memory
- emotional self-regulation
- reconstitution

Behavioral Inhibition

Behavioral inhibition describes the ability to control attention, thoughts, and actions so that a person can override his immediate desires and predisposition. This capacity depends on three processes—the ability to delay one's response to an event, to interrupt an ongoing response to an event, and to prevent interference from competing events. Without this capacity, a person will focus on the *immediate* consequences of any action or behavior and fail to develop capacity for self-control. Behavioral inhibition is foundational to the development and maturation of the other executive functions.

What challenges might a child or teen who struggles with behavioral inhibition experience when their parents or caregivers bring them to church services or programs? They will find it more difficult than their peers to keep impulsive or aggressive behavior in check. They may have more difficulty sitting, standing, or kneeling for an extended time, especially when they become bored.

And what about adults who struggle with behavioral inhibition? They set the alarm clock on Saturday night with good intentions of getting up early to take the family to church, but climb back into bed after looking out the window and experiencing the temperature contrast between their cold room and warm bed.

Verbal Working Memory

Verbal working memory involves the capacity to use words to represent thoughts or actions and to keep those words and thoughts at the forefront of one's mind. The ability to hold and reflect on a thought without having to say the thought aloud enables children to *internalize* rules of behavior. Moral development largely depends on this capacity. Verbal working memory allows children and adults to reflect on their conduct and behavior. The ability of children to pray silently serves as evidence this capacity is developing appropriately.

Children with weaknesses in verbal working memory may experience frustration or embarrassment in attempting to memorize Scripture or prayers. They aren't winning prizes at AWANA or getting picked for the church's "Bible Jeopardy" team. Memorizing an act of contrition can be a daunting task to a second grader preparing for the sacrament of reconciliation with a priest in a Roman Catholic parish.

Teens and adults with weaknesses in verbal working memory may struggle to apply principles from Scripture and lessons from sermons or homilies in their daily lives. Knowledge acquired in one setting may not generalize to other settings. For example, a teen may be unable to apply last week's study of Matthew 18 in resolving a conflict with a peer in youth group. They may ramble or experience frustration in communicating their main point in a small group or in a Bible study. They often aggravate pastors, group leaders, and fellow attendees at church events, who may perceive them as "talking too much."

Nonverbal Working Memory

Nonverbal working memory refers to the capacity to maintain and recall a *picture of events* in the forefront of one's mind. It is foundational to the ability to recognize recurring patterns when analyzing problems or situations and enables a child or adult to predict future events. This capacity allows us to rehearse actions and behaviors, anticipate the consequences of actions, manage relationships, and plan complex, goal-directed behavior. Moral conduct and social cooperation rely on this capacity.

Kids, teens, and adults with weaknesses in nonverbal working memory may struggle to arrive on time to various church activities. They tend to underestimate the time required to complete routine tasks, like getting ready for church or driving a certain distance. When my wife served as a children's ministry greeter at our church, she often observed children or parents with this weakness hopping across the parking lot with one shoe on ten minutes after the beginning of the service. Kids may become frustrated by their inability to master hand gestures that often accompany music in children's worship services. Kids tend to leave the paper with the dinner table discussion questions from their Sunday school lesson in their classrooms or misplace handouts in their Bibles.

Adults with nonverbal memory challenges may become frustrated while searching for rooms or activities in a building. They are often described as having a poor sense of direction—struggling to visualize directions or needing to have directions repeated to them multiple times. Their forgetfulness is greater for tasks and activities that are outside their daily routines. They forget their Bibles at home or leave required permission forms for their teen's youth ministry retreat at the spot on the kitchen counter where they signed them. They're scrambling to do the required reading for their small group or Bible study while riding in the car to their church activity.

Emotional Self-regulation

Emotional self-regulation involves the capacity to keep private one's initial response to an event or situation. This capacity allows a person to modify their response to an event and the emotions that accompany their response. It also helps moderate the intensity with which children and adults experience emotion. Relaxation strategies may be thought of as exercises designed to reinforce and strengthen capacity for emotional regulation. This capacity is necessary for adults to keep their jobs when frustrated by a supervisor. It also helps drivers stay out of jail when pulled over by a police officer for speeding!

Children and teens who are delayed in their development of this capacity will often be viewed by adults as disrespectful and defiant and by their peers as immature. They may be prone to tantrums or meltdowns in the absence of apparent provocation. Pastors, church staff members, and volunteers may not get the opportunity to observe the behavior in question, because families of children who struggle with emotional self-regulation *may never get out the door to head to church.* By the end of a long week, parents are often so worn down by the effort involved in getting their child to school that they avoid the conflict likely to result from trying to compel the child to get ready for church. If they're successful in getting their child out the door and into the car, the anger and frustration expressed during the ride to church may affect the parents' ability to enter with a worshipful mind-set.

Adults who struggle with emotional self-regulation are often prone to interpersonal conflicts at church. They may openly express frustration with aspects of church they don't like (the pastor, the teaching, the music, for example) through inappropriate channels at inappropriate times. Parents may become indignant when children's ministry volunteers refuse to release their child after worship without the ticket they received at check-in. They may develop a reputation in the church for failing to keep long-term commitments.

Emotional self-regulation is closely associated with motivation. Our ability to set long-term goals, to delay gratification, and to maintain the self-discipline necessary to achieve long-term goals in the absence of immediate rewards and reinforcement is highly dependent on this capacity. Teens and adults who fail to develop sufficient capacity for emotional self-regulation will struggle to maintain a spiritually disciplined life.

Reconstitution

The easiest way for me to describe the concept of reconstitution is to compare this function to a digital video recorder housed within the mind. It involves the ability to use private visual imagery and language to replay and analyze past events to glean more information from those events and better understand the causes and effects of specific outcomes.

For a mental image of someone using reconstitution in daily life, think of a football coach watching game film of his own team and also of his team's upcoming opponent. A diligent coach might look at film frame by frame to try to understand why some plays worked and others didn't, to identify the techniques and strategies his most recent opponent used effectively to thwart his game plan, to spot tendencies in the upcoming opponent's substitution patterns and play calling in different game situations, and to imagine new strategies for exploiting his next opponent's weaknesses.

Reconstitution is another way of describing our capacity for creativity and problem solving. It allows us to visualize and mentally rehearse different approaches to solving problems without having to test each possible approach or solution in real life. A child or adult having a hard time with reconstitution may struggle in resolving conflicts with peers or leaders, managing schedule conflicts between church and outside commitments, or strategizing the best way to approach church leaders with a pressing need.

■ ■ ■

Before we move to the sensory processing barrier, let's look at the relationship between executive functioning deficiencies and specific mental health conditions and review how environmental factors compound mental illness-related deficiencies.

Persons with executive functioning difficulties experience them as either a core feature or a consequence of conditions described at the beginning of this section. Executive functioning weakness has been hypothesized to represent the core difference in brain function among persons with ADHD, and these weaknesses are very common in persons with autism spectrum disorders.[2] Also, children and adults with depression or mania struggle with executive functioning during acute mood episodes.

Neuroimaging studies in patients with schizophrenia consistently demonstrate a loss of brain tissue in regions of the prefrontal cortex vital to executive functioning. This phenomenon is associated with the marked difficulty some persons with schizophrenia experience in following through on tasks of daily living and self-care.

Executive functioning is often compromised by fetal exposure to alcohol, drugs, and other toxins and is adversely effected by the effects of stress hormones and neural pathways activated in response to adverse childhood experiences, including trauma and abuse.[3]

Executive functioning weakness represents a quality of disability often seen in persons currently served in special needs ministries. Executive functioning may be greatly compromised in children, teens, and adults with intellectual or developmental disabilities. In fact, many of the church consultation requests we receive at Key Ministry have to do with challenges with self-control in youth with intellectual disabilities.

In chapter 1, I referred to the "all-or-nothing" thinking—Can they or can't they control it?—that is common among parents and church leaders in understanding disruptive behavior. I shared that most children and adults with executive functioning deficits have some capacity to control their emotions and behavior, but they expend far more mental energy and effort to maintain control compared to their same-age peers. Capacity for self-control is often highly dependent on their level of interest in the task at hand and the characteristics of the environments in which they find themselves.

It's helpful to have a framework for understanding how and why executive functioning is affected by the qualities of one's surroundings. One way to grasp the challenge they face is to think of their brain as an older computer lacking the memory or processing power to do everything it needs to when many applications are running all at once. They may have the raw processing power to do what they need to do when there are only two or three apps running, but when they try to run fifteen at the same time, the system crashes. The computer just stops functioning, and the dreaded pinwheel (for Mac users) or spinning hourglass (for Windows users) appears on the screen. The more environmental input and sensory stimulation the brain is compelled to process, the less capacity is available to devote to the most important tasks in the moment.

You've probably heard that folks with emotional or behavioral challenges benefit from "structure." What is structure, and why is structure helpful to someone who struggles with executive functioning? When we establish clear routines, reduce or eliminate potential sources of distraction, and minimize the time and effort required for decision making, the child or adult has more cognitive capacity to focus on the most important tasks in that moment.

THE FOURTH BARRIER: SENSORY PROCESSING

Sensory processing disorder (SPD) is not currently recognized as a stand-alone medical condition, but sensory processing difficulties are common among children and teens with autism spectrum disorders, ADHD, and anxiety disorders. Five percent or more of children and teens in the United States experience significant functional impairment because of abnormal sensory processing.[4]

A neuroimaging study done by investigators from the University of California in San Francisco demonstrated quantifiable differences in brain structure among children with sensory processing disorder. This finding helped to establish a biological basis for distinguishing the condition from other neurodevelopmental disorders.[5]

Persons with sensory processing differences become overwhelmed because of difficulty integrating too much or too little incoming information from their senses—sight, smell, touch, hearing, and taste. The condition was first described by an occupational therapist who recognized two additional sources of sensory input originating within the body—*proprioception* (our unconscious awareness of body position and movement, contributing to posture and motor control) and *vestibular* input (contributing to balance, spatial orientation, and coordination) associated with functional impairment.[6]

Children and adults who are *hypersensitive* often demonstrate marked aversion to noise, light, touch, and taste. They may be very particular about the feel of clothes against their skin, pull away in response to touch, experience pain in the presence of loud noise, or become nauseous around persons who are wearing strong perfume or cologne. They may appear to be clumsy, are prone to bumping into objects and people, and avoid gross motor activities involving strength, balance, or coordination.

Children who are *hyposensitive* may be thought of as sensory seekers. They love tight hugs, physical contact, amusement park rides, trampolines, climbing, jumping, and splashing. They may also have a hard time sitting still and keeping their hands to themselves at a worship service or church activity.

Your inclusion team will need to develop a strategy to welcome children and adults with these sensory processing differences into church events. In some instances, church members and visitors may demonstrate hypersensitivity to some types of sensory input and hyposensitivity to others at the same time.

Now that we've recognized why persons with heightened reactivity to sensory stimulation experience our ministry environments differently, let's consider how they might be challenged by a range of church experiences and activities.*

Arriving at Church

Churches are busy places on Sunday mornings. Lots of people crowd together within confined spaces near entrances and exits before and after worship services. Both the level of ambient noise and the experience of multiple conversations taking place at once near the person with sensory processing differences are likely to produce distress. Physical proximity results in lots of bumping and touching. Some children with a "fight or flight" response may run away or be at risk of meltdowns in response to sensory overload.

Attending a Worship Service

Many churches offer high-energy worship experiences with loud music and bright lights. While this worship style may work well for some persons with sensory hyposensitivity and can help capture and maintain the attention of children and adults who spend much of their week preoccupied by electronic devices, persons with high sensitivity to sensory stimulation may experience intense discomfort in this type of service. Having to sit for an extended time in uncomfortable seating may be a major challenge for some children and adults. In Catholic churches, use of incense during the Mass; the need to sit, stand, or kneel throughout the Mass; and the expectation for worshipers to exchanges handshakes as a sign of peace with others in their immediate area are potential sources of distress.

Going to Special Events

A Vacation Bible School experience often combines high levels of physical activity with high levels of sensory stimulation. Children and adults with hypersensitivity may avoid church festivals and carnivals,

---

* Note that in chapter 9, we'll discusses various approaches for making our churches more sensory-friendly for children and adults with sensory processing differences.

along with weekend retreats held at outdoor campsites and mission trips to locations where the comforts of home aren't readily available.

THE FIFTH BARRIER: SOCIAL COMMUNICATION

Churches are intensely social places. In *The Purpose Driven Life*, Rick Warren identifies community as one of the five purposes for which we were created—community with God and community with one another.[7] Pastor and author Max Lucado has also taught about the importance of community in church life:

> Christ distributes courage through community; he dissipates doubts through fellowship. He never deposits all knowledge in one person but distributes pieces of the jigsaw puzzle to many. When you interlock your understanding with mine, and we share our discoveries . . . When we mix, mingle, confess, and pray, Christ speaks.[8]

The biblical emphasis on living in Christian community in relationships with others in the body of Christ permeates and shapes the calendar of the local church—as it should! Our growth as followers of Christ happens in a group, not merely as individuals (1 Corinthians 12:14–27). We gather together at least once a week for worship. Many of our children and young adults attend Christian schools and universities, where they spend much of their day surrounded by peers being raised in the faith or seeking to grow in faith. In many churches—Protestant and Roman Catholic alike—children, teens, and adults are expected to actively participate in a small group. We're encouraged to serve alongside one another in community outreach and missions. But I suspect most pastors and church leaders have never considered what church might be like for someone who struggles with social interactions.

Challenges with social communication are common among persons with a broad range of mental health and developmental disabilities. The need for support with social communication is one of the two defining features of autism spectrum disorders as defined in the *DSM-5*. Social communication is often a major source of functional impairment among persons with psychotic disorders (including schizophrenia), ADHD, anxiety disorders, and pragmatic language disorders.

I'll share many ideas in a later chapter for welcoming and including persons who have social communication challenges, but let's first consider why attending church may be difficult for a child or adult with social skill deficits:

- If someone has difficulty in making or keeping friends, how likely is it that they'll know someone in your congregation who will invite them to church?
- How many social interactions will they need to navigate the first time they visit your church with potential for causing embarrassment?
- How might a child or teen react if they come to a church activity and encounter peers who bully them outside of church—at school, in extracurricular activities, or through social media?
- How would your church members respond to someone who doesn't follow social convention regarding appearance or dress, or someone who struggles to follow common rules of social behavior, such as knowing when to speak or how to take turns while speaking?
- What challenges might a teen or adult with less mature social skills encounter if they're expected to attend a Bible study or small group with unfamiliar people in an unfamiliar place?
- What obstacles might they face if they want to volunteer in ways that make the best use of their gifts and talents?

Sydney* is a young adult who contacted Key Ministry in response to a blog post on social communication. She granted me permission to share her experiences of church as a person diagnosed with Asperger syndrome, ADHD, depression, and anxiety. Her story typifies the struggles adults with social communication difficulties encounter at church:

I have managed to alienate everyone at my old church—apparently through breaking countless social rules, though I'm not sure which ones. It is hard to know what I do wrong since no one communicates with me and I cannot read body language. Even when I try to send update emails, I get no response. It is so hard for me to initiate conversations. Therefore, I even sent an email with pictures from Corinth and Ephesus to initiate a conversation. However, no one from church ever emailed me back...

I do not want to join a small group in a new church because I am so afraid of becoming alienated again. My old pastor told me I just needed to get more antidepressants and more friends—if only it was that easy. In my old church, I tried doing Alpha at the church, but I never felt like I was part of the fellowship. I enjoyed watching the Alpha videos online more.

When I have autistic meltdowns, worries, or compulsions, I am just admonished for not giving things to God and that I have not asked for enough healing. If I speak about issues such as modesty, they admonish me for being too shy, introverted, or antisocial. In discussions, I'm admonished for always being too off topic. Do not even get me started sitting still for quiet time with God. Clear sermons with pictures and outlines are such a blessing (though church with so much socializing can be tiring)!

I applied to several Christian schools, but I have found them to be the least accepting of my disabilities. I have this vision that if I ever get married, it will be an empty church.

---

* Her name has been changed to protect her identity.

I do not even know how to approach joining a church now since it is so evident that no one at my old church in my old city wants anything to do with me. For all the talk on forgiveness, I am apparently too eccentric and egocentric to be forgiven and to be accepted. Moreover, if not even loving Christians can put up with me, the rest of the world seems scary.

THE SIXTH BARRIER: SOCIAL ISOLATION

Evangelists have observed that churches experiencing the largest increases in membership through conversion rely on very different approaches in sharing the gospel from those employed by preceding generations of pastors and church leaders. As Christ followers pour love out on those who have not yet come to faith and invite them to take part in the community available through the church, seekers will discover why they should accept the claims the Bible makes about Jesus and will come to faith in him. People first need to feel they *belong* before they will *believe*.[9]

The well-known pastor, author, and blogger Carey Nieuwhof believes that *personal invitations* will be the primary way non-Christians will come to worship services in the future.[10] Where will that leave individuals and families who may not know anyone who will invite them to church?

Our sixth barrier—social isolation—is discussed immediately following social communication because they overlap. Social communication represents one attribute of mental illness contributing to social isolation. But there are many factors beyond social communication that contribute to the social isolation that is all too common among families impacted by mental illness.

When I think about the kids and families we serve in our practice, a list of common causes for social isolation quickly comes to mind. Let's look at a few of the more significant causes:

Unavailability of Appropriate Child Care

We've noted that kids with mental health conditions are more likely to struggle with self-control, anxiety, and emotional regulation. Because their parents often can't depend on teens in the neighborhood with little training or experience to watch their children, they have a hard time getting out of the house to connect with other parents or couples. A study conducted by the Massachusetts Department of Mental Health reported that only 17.6 percent of families of children with mental illness were accessing respite care—child care offered by trained providers to provide relief for the caregivers. More than 64 percent of families were unable to find anyone to provide respite care, and for more than half of the families surveyed, the respite care available to them was unaffordable.[11] Even when child care is available, it may be too expensive. Discretionary income is often limited in families affected by mental illness because of expenses for therapy or medication not covered by health insurance—if the family can afford health insurance.

Exclusion from Christian Schools

Children with a broad range of disability (including mental health conditions) who could be included in traditional classroom settings with appropriate accommodations or support services are significantly less likely to attend Christian schools.[12] Despite the efforts of organizations such as CLC (Christian Learning Center) Network to help Christian schools implement disability inclusion, a recent study reported that 95 percent of accredited "Christ-centered" schools in California don't accept children with disabilities.[13] In churches that operate a school, the school often serves as a hub of social activity. When children and teens can't attend the school because of a disability, the child misses out on a peer group that could help assimilate into the church and parents are left without a social network of families with common interests in church involvement and spiritual development that could provide mutual encouragement and support.

Involvement in Youth Sports

This cause of social isolation also represents an opportunity for churches looking to increase attendance at weekend worship services. Kids with mental illness are less likely to be part of the youth sports culture through which parents connect with families with common interests. Difficulties with motor coordination occur more frequently in kids with mental health disorders or developmental disabilities.[14] In my experience, children and teens with ADHD and anxiety disorders often experience more difficulty than their peers in maintaining commitments to team sports. In many churches, participation on church-sponsored teams affords another opportunity for social networking and interaction. Kids who are unable to attend a church-affiliated school because of their educational support needs are more likely to lack the athletic skills necessary to thrive in competitive team sports.

Lack of Friendships

Individuals with mental health conditions often rub peers the wrong way. A boy with ADHD who is too impatient to follow the rules of a game or who struggles to control his temper is less likely to be invited for playdates, birthday parties, and special events than his peers. A kid who can't get invited to a birthday party won't get invited to Vacation Bible School. A bright teen or adult with an autism spectrum disorder may find himself sitting alone in the cafeteria or lunchroom after peers become frustrated by his incessant conversation about trivial football statistics. Acquaintances of a young woman with social anxiety may stop texting or calling after she declines invitations to parties, concerts, or other large groups activities. As I've noted previously, persons with depression or anxiety may intentionally distance themselves from others because of discomfort resulting from their mental health condition.

The Bible instructs us that we are to *go* and make disciples (Matthew 28:19)—a directive that is especially relevant when it comes to sharing the gospel with persons with mental illness, because the nature of their condition makes it less likely that they will seek out a church or know someone within a church who is inclined to invite them to church activities.

THE SEVENTH BARRIER: FAMILY EXPERIENCES OF CHURCH

I've never hunted, golfed, or gone skiing, even though a fair number of my friends and neighbors engage in these activities on a regular basis. Why don't I do those things? My family didn't participate in any of those activities when I was a kid. I did, however, play baseball, football, and basketball and regularly attended college and professional games as a spectator. My father was an outstanding amateur baseball player in his youth. He taught me the game at an early age and served as a public address announcer for the home football and basketball games of the large public university located in the city where I grew up. My experiences working in the press box alongside my dad probably explain why I've been a season ticket holder as an adult for each of our professional sports teams here in Cleveland—if the Browns can be considered a professional team.

Our families impart interests, habits, hobbies, and experiences that shape the traditions and experiences we in turn share with our own children, and church attendance represents a vitally important habit and tradition for Christian families. I don't go golfing or hunting because my dad never taught me to golf or hunt. My guess is that many of my friends and neighbors who don't attend church came from families where their parents didn't take them to church. In looking at why individuals and families impacted by mental illness don't go to church, the family's past experiences of church may explain their continued absence from worship services and other activities.

One factor influencing a family's history of church involvement is the *multigenerational expression of many common mental health conditions.* A common observation in my practice is that the apple doesn't fall far from the tree. Some mental health conditions are highly heritable. Roughly one in three children of parents who have schizophrenia, bipolar disorder, or depression will develop a serious mental illness—and not necessarily the same mental illness as their parent.[15] A parental history of anxiety (especially maternal history) contributes to a twofold to sevenfold increase in the risk for anxiety in their offspring.[16]

Because my focus professionally is in treating kids with mental health conditions and my work through Key Ministry in connecting churches and families of children with disabilities involves children and student ministry leaders, my initial thoughts about a mental health inclusion strategy centered around the needs of children and teens. But any strategies to include kids with mental illness at church must also address the obstacles a child's *parents* or *caregivers* may experience in association with *their own mental health issues.* After all, if Mom or Dad doesn't attend church, it's highly unlikely that their kids will be coming to church. If a child experiences mental health concerns that keep them from church, there's a reasonable possibility that their mother or father experienced similar difficulties that kept them from attending church. Most kids aren't old enough to drive themselves to church, and the ones who are old enough won't drive themselves if no one has ever taken them to church.

The second factor affecting family involvement involves past interactions with pastors, church staff, and volunteers when mental health-related challenges have arisen at church. When a parent raised with a strong faith in Christ has a bad church experience resulting from the church's response to a child with a disability, the family will often seek another church that is better prepared to address their child's needs. But what happens when someone who lacks a strong faith foundation experiences a problem at church related to their own mental health disability or a family member's mental health challenges? For them to give church another try, they'll likely need lots of evidence that their next experience will be different.

▪ ▪ ▪

Over the last two chapters, I've identified seven common barriers to church involvement for children and adults with mental illness and their families and pointed out how attributes and qualities associated with common and serious mental health disorders create difficulties at church. Now that we've identified the problem, we need to develop a strategy for addressing it. In the next and final chapter of part 1, I'll introduce seven components of a comprehensive church inclusion strategy designed to welcome all persons impacted by mental illness to your worship services and ministry events.

FIVE

What Can Churches
Do to Help?

In the last two chapters, we identified seven barriers that frequently impede children and adults with mental illness from attending church-sponsored activities like weekend worship services, small group meetings, Bible study sessions, overnight retreats, mission trips, and volunteer opportunities. In this chapter, I'll introduce a process to help your church's leadership team or the leadership team of your ministry area to develop a plan to minimize and overcome these barriers to inclusion.

Mental health inclusion is best understood as a mind-set for doing ministry rather than a "program" for ministry. You'll soon discover the unique challenges each person or family impacted by mental illness experiences in attending worship services and other church activities and recognize the difficulty in developing a program capable of accommodating *everyone* in your surrounding community who struggles to attend church. The seven inclusion strategies I'll share are sufficiently comprehensive to guide mental health inclusion efforts in large churches with multiple campuses, yet flexible enough to be useful for churches of all sizes. Each strategy may not apply to *all* of the barriers I described in the preceding chapters, but taken together, the strategies represent a paradigm to guide your church team in implementing an inclusion plan across each of your ministries.

The seven strategies I'll introduce in this chapter form the acronym TEACHER—I hope this helps you remember them!

T: Assemble your inclusion *TEAM*.

E: Create welcoming ministry *ENVIRONMENTS*.

A: Focus on ministry *ACTIVITIES* most essential for spiritual growth.

C: *COMMUNICATE* effectively.

H: *HELP* families with their most heartfelt needs.

E: Offer *EDUCATION* and support.

R: Empower your people to assume *RESPONSIBILITY* for ministry.

Before beginning your mental health inclusion initiative, there's one essential task you'll need to complete.

Do you remember *City Slickers*—the now classic movie starring Billy Crystal? In the film, Curly, an old cowboy magnificently played by Jack Palance, and Mitch, played by Crystal, are riding their horses on the trail. Curly turns to Mitch and asks him if he knows what the secret of life is. Mitch says no, and Curly holds up one finger and says, "This." Mitch says, "Your finger?" And Curly answers with a simple phrase: "One thing. Just one thing."

When it comes to a strategy for inclusion, I have found that there is "one thing"—other than God's blessing, presence, and ongoing wisdom—that is *essential* to the success of a mental health inclusion ministry. Any mental health inclusion initiative is doomed to failure without *the unequivocal support of your senior pastor.*

A reality of most church cultures is that the ministries and initiatives that receive the necessary commitment of time, money, and volunteer resources are those that matter most to senior leadership. Saddleback Church is a nationwide leader in supporting mental health ministry. Why? Because the ministry is important to their senior pastor, Rick Warren, and his wife, Kay. Their son Matthew experienced recurrent episodes of severe depression for many years before ultimately committing suicide. Because of their personal concern about this issue, mental health ministry has become a priority for their church as well.

I suspect that many of you reading this book and looking for help on this ministry adventure are church members or lay leaders who sense a call to welcome children, adults, and families impacted by mental illness into your home church. That's great! However, if you're seeking to start a mental health inclusion initiative and your job title is something other than senior pastor, your number one job is to get senior leadership to buy into the plan. The first step could be to share this book with your senior pastor or to set up an informal meeting with him or her to discuss the key concepts.

But let me advise you to be patient and discerning as well. Consider why your pastor or church staff may have reservations about this type of initiative. Implementing even the most *minor* change in church routines or practices often presents enormous challenges to church staff. If you don't believe me, ask a pastor or staff member from your church about the volume of complaints they receive about the worship music, the preacher's outfit, the coffee, or the donut selection—small details or inconveniences most people never notice. If leadership hasn't fully bought into your inclusion ministry initiative, they won't be willing to work through the inevitable pushback resulting from even tiny modifications to ministry practices or environments. You may need to be patient. Change may not come as quickly as you would like. Be gracious and understanding in your communication with your church leaders.

Another reality of church culture is that most churches have far more ministry opportunities than they have resources. When you meet with your pastor or senior leadership team, be prepared to address unspoken concerns about the potential for your initiative to draw volunteers and financial support from established ministries that depend on those resources. Nothing makes a church staff member or ministry leader more defensive than the prospect of losing a key volunteer. Support from senior leadership will be essential for overcoming reservations among staff or volunteers responsible for the other ministries of the church.

If you feel led to champion the launch of a mental health inclusion initiative and find your church's leadership team doesn't immediately support your proposal, I implore you to avoid leaping to the conclusion that your church's leaders are disobedient to God. The pastors and church leaders I've come to know put more thought and prayer into discerning God's will for maximizing the impact of their ministries than most attendees will ever know.

With that said, this inclusion model was designed for churches with diverse cultures, management styles, denominational traditions, worship styles, and ministry philosophies. Our model anticipates the most significant objections of church leaders in a wide range of settings.[1] Our model is designed to work in churches with relatively few stand-alone ministries but is easily adapted for churches that offer a wide range of excellent ministry programs.

This chapter introduces each of the seven strategies for overcoming barriers to inclusion of individuals and families impacted by mental illness. In part 2, I'll focus on specific ways in which each strategy can be applied across the ministries of your church to surmount the barriers to church involvement. Consider this chapter to be an owner's manual to the tool kit you'll be using to build your churchwide inclusion initiative.

STRATEGY #1: ASSEMBLE YOUR TEAM

If you were to have the task of putting together a dream team to lead your church's mental health ministry, stop to consider who you might include and where you might look (both inside and outside your church) for people with the gifts, talents, knowledge, and experiences necessary to implement effective outreach and inclusion across all your church's ministries.

As we discussed earlier in this chapter, even if your senior pastor isn't the first member of your team, he or she must publicly support your initiative. They may not need to be involved in every team meeting or communication moving forward (especially in a large church), but they do need to endorse your ministry's overall goals and strategies. The senior pastor has the necessary influence to engage staff and volunteers in your plans. I'm far more likely to respond to a need if my senior pastor asks me to get involved than I would be if I were contacted by a junior staff member or a volunteer. Your senior pastor will very likely be the most effective recruiter for your ministry team.

Next, enlist a representative from all the major ministry departments to help implement a mental health inclusion plan—basically, get everybody involved! As you explore the other inclusion strategies in this chapter, you'll appreciate the need to involve many different leaders or teams in your planning process, recognizing that in many small churches, many of these ministries or functions don't exist, or in some instances, individual leaders are responsible for multiple functions. Here's a list of possible ministries from which to recruit a representative:

- your teaching team
- your worship team
- your assimilation team/greeters
- your children's, student, youth, and family ministry teams
- your adult ministry team
- your small group ministry team
- your communications team
- your facilities maintenance team
- your counseling ministry team
- your medical ministry team
- your disability/special needs ministry team

Once you've established your core team of staff members/ministry leaders who will form your team's foundation, you will want them to nominate and invite other team members who may or may not attend your church with unique gifts, talents, knowledge, or expertise for your inclusion process. Your church will likely include members or attendees with valuable professional training or life experiences. These individuals include the following:

Mental health professionals. The picture that comes to mind when I mention mental health professionals likely includes people with advanced degrees and lots of training—psychiatrists, psychologists, counselors, social workers, or advanced practice nurses. If you're leading an initiative in a small church or a small community where mental health treatment resources are scarce, expand your playing field. Consider support staff from clinics, schools, and public agencies where mental health services are provided. Team members with backgrounds in mental health will help your church staff and volunteers anticipate the challenges the people they serve may experience if they seek to attend your church. They'll also have a keen appreciation for the challenges their clients face in navigating the tasks of daily living. Don't overlook the receptionists, billing clerks, and case managers who work in mental health clinics. They're positioned to help families connect with your church if the mental health practitioners who hold professional degrees fail to recognize the benefits of directing families to the church for spiritual comfort or tangible support.

Mental health advocates. Church members who have personal experience of mental illness or a parent or caregiver of a child with mental illness offer a vital perspective to your team. Members or attendees actively involved with the National Alliance for Mental Illness (NAMI) or other mental health advocacy organizations have relationships with individuals and families in your local community who need a welcoming and supportive church, and they'll have lots of practical ideas for providing support to persons in your community impacted by mental illness.

Occupational therapists. Sensory processing differences are common among children and adults with a broad range of mental health conditions. Occupational therapists generally have more experience than professionals from other disciplines in addressing challenges that arise in persons with enhanced sensitivity to light, noise, smell, taste, and touch and are likely to have useful suggestions for modifying ministry environments to be welcoming for persons with sensory processing issues.

Interior designers. The physical spaces in which ministry takes place should promote communication, social engagement, and activity leading to a desired spiritual outcome. Qualities of our ministry environments that may go relatively unnoticed by many attendees—seating, lighting, signage, fixtures, furniture, and the use of color—frequently impact the experience of persons with common mental health conditions. Good design may increase the likelihood that attendees will remember the senior pastor's sermon the following day, decrease the anxiety of a first-time attendee, and promote self-control in kids with impulsive behavior. An experienced interior designer armed with an understanding of your ministry activities and a little education on challenges posed by common mental health conditions may offer useful and inexpensive suggestions for making your ministry environments more welcoming.

Social workers. Recruit persons who have a background in social services or case management or who are familiar with local agencies and resources that serve children and adults impacted by mental illness. They may have connections with families serving in your local adoption and foster care systems—systems serving a disproportionate number of children and youth with mental health concerns. Team members familiar with your local social service system can help families of children and adults with a range of challenges like finding good mental health care, housing, job training, and employment services. Individuals with mental illness often need help in navigating educational or insurance bureaucracies. Connecting families from your church with much-needed community support services is a tangible blessing your church can extend to the mental health community. Get at least one of these social services experts on your team!

Wise laypersons. Look for a spiritually mature church member who has firsthand experience of mental illness or simply a spiritually mature parent of a child or teen affected by mental illness or trauma. Research suggests that families impacted by mental illness greatly value the support of their local church.[2] Someone from your church who has lived with mental illness or has reared a child with mental illness or trauma exposure will have unique insights to share with your team as to how the church can most effectively serve persons in your congregation and community impacted by mental illness.

You'll likely include others on your team with unique gifts and talents beyond members with relevant professional backgrounds and life experience. You might consider persons for your team who are rarely asked to serve in the church or who may not even profess faith in Christ. At Key Ministry, we were approached by a psychologist (and a self-proclaimed atheist) who offered to train volunteers in churches we were serving free of charge because he was so impressed with the support the churches were providing to families from the school where he worked. By doing this work, you may create opportunities to influence nonbelievers and discover hidden gifts and talents in your church, which God intended for your inclusion ministry. As the apostle Paul wrote, "For just as each of us has one body with many members, and these members do not all have the same function, so in Christ we, though many, form one body, and each member belongs to all the others. We have different gifts, according to the grace given to each of us" (Romans 12:4–6).

STRATEGY #2: CREATE WELCOMING MINISTRY ENVIRONMENTS

I will admit that I have very little knowledge of interior design. "Form follows function" is the extent of my knowledge, a phrase that simply means that whatever the purpose of a space is—the function—the interior design should support that purpose. This principle is important for churches to consider if they want to create the best possible experience for guests and attendees with common mental conditions.

Imagine that your church decides to build a new facility or renovate your existing ministry space. When your church leaders interview prospective architects, the architect will likely ask lots of questions about the intended uses of each space. I suspect most church leaders have never considered how children and adults with common mental illnesses experience differently the physical spaces where ministry takes place than other attendees do. Since fifty million people in the United States have a mental disorder at any one time, creating spaces that promote the purposes of the ministry taking place within that space for all people should be an important consideration. Form follows function.

An easy way to observe this principle in practice is to take a trip to your local shopping center and visit a few stores operated by nationally successful retailers. Every aspect of the store's layout and design advances the purpose of separating shoppers from their money. The window displays will feature merchandise in as flattering a manner as possible, sometimes with a little help from Photoshop. Retailers employ lighting, color, and music, along with strategically positioned merchandise, to draw attention to the items the store most wants to sell and to create an image in the shopper's mind that differentiates their "brand" from others and cultivates loyalty among customers.

North Point Ministries in metropolitan Atlanta serves as a model of a church that plans and designs facilities strategically in support of a well-defined mission to create churches that unchurched people love to attend. When I've had opportunities to visit different North Point campuses, I've come away impressed by their thoughtfulness in creating spaces for their children, youth, and adults that promote the ministry taking place within.

At any North Point church, the children's ministry areas share a common look intended to promote a sense of wonder, discovery, and passion among kids taking part in their programming. Adult worship spaces are set up to minimize distraction during services and complement a teaching style designed to help attendees remember *one actionable truth* from the message. North Point's senior pastor (Andy Stanley) wrote an entire book describing how the church developed a communication strategy to overcome the propensity to distraction he observed among church attendees.[3] The book's first chapter is titled "No One's Listening."

I remember on one of my trips to Atlanta visiting a friend who worked at a North Point satellite campus located in a large commercial office building and being struck by the ease with which I could follow the signage inside the parking deck and the entryways to the church to find exactly where I needed to go. I came away from my visit thinking that the North Point team had (probably unintentionally) designed a church to welcome children and adults with ADHD. The visit had sparked my interest in how churches might create ministry environments that families impacted by other mental health conditions might find appealing.

I've met enough pastors to understand how much thought and planning goes into the design of worship services or the weekly activities in children's or student ministry. Church members become quite attached to—and are often very opinionated about—their preferences in worship music or church architecture. I'm not making value judgments about one style of worship service or church architecture over another. Successful mental health inclusion doesn't require your church to adopt contemporary worship if your people haven't embraced that style or to build a new building! But I will challenge you to consider how your church can make your ministry environments more welcoming to kids and teens with common mental health conditions and their families, regardless of their current state or design.

Let's start by thinking about how people with some of the traits I described in the last chapter experience the spaces where worship, education, and fellowship take place in your church. How would the experience of a child or adult who struggles with distraction differ from that of other attendees? Consider the spaces in your church where the most important teaching occurs. Is there anything in those spaces that is likely to interfere with the ability of all attendees to process and absorb the teaching and to retain the content? Are there windows in the room? Is there a need for curtains or blinds? Can curtains or blinds be adjusted to minimize distraction during teaching activities? What about the wall decorations and artwork? Do they support the functions taking place within that space or contribute to distraction? Do the objects hanging in your sanctuary represent a help or hindrance for attendees as they prepare themselves for worship?

Researchers from Carnegie Mellon University have published a fascinating study that has implications for how decorations could be used in spaces used for children's ministry programming.[4] In their study, they noted that kindergarteners retained less information from a science lesson and experienced more challenges with self-control in classrooms with more wall decorations.

Consider the seating in your worship spaces and rooms set aside for education. Is it comfortable? Do your seats serve as a source of distraction or discomfort? If young children are expected to attend services with their families, are there resources for parents who are preoccupied throughout the service with preventing their children from becoming a source of distraction? Do attendees dwell on feeling too hot or too cold at the expense of the message being communicated by your pastors, teachers, and ministry leaders?

Signage is another important component of your ministry environments. As we learned in the last chapter, many common mental health conditions impact the ability to remember and recall multistep instructions. Make sure that your signs and directions are clear and simple. This starts with your parking lot. A Key Ministry blog reader shared the following observations:

> As someone with ADD and a history of anxiety/depression, I wish I could impress how simple and effective it is to clearly communicate traffic patterns, church campus and parking entrances and parking directions with signage—even mapped on websites . . .

I've visited churches and left before reaching the parking lot if the traffic was overly stimulating and the parking lot was confusing and poorly marked. I've turned around in a parking lot if I couldn't find the correct entrance after parking and leaving my car. Imagine having a panic attack with a car of family, forcing yourself to go in while wanting to cry in the bathroom—avoidable with clear signs and a good map on a website.[5]

Your church's exterior and interior signs should avoid insider lingo. A visitor to my church, for example, would likely have no idea that our large group children's ministry programming is called "Upstreet" or that signs for "Circle of Friends" direct them to our special needs ministry.

Welcoming ministry environments for kids and adults with mental illness are likely to be sensory friendly. In the last chapter, we learned that sensory processing differences are common among persons with ADHD, anxiety disorders, and autism spectrum disorders and result in enhanced sensitivity to sound, light, touch, and taste. Children with sensory processing differences often become defiant when parents insist they go to church. Adults with these differences resist invitations to church. I'll devote an entire chapter to sensory-friendly ministry environments in the second part of the book.

Finally, I encourage you to consider how your ministry environments support children and adults predisposed to struggle with impulse control. In the last chapter, we explored the ways in which executive functioning—the set of cognitive abilities involved in controlling and regulating other abilities and behaviors—is affected across a broad range of mental health conditions. We also observed that most persons who struggle with executive functioning (outside of a severe episode of mental illness) retain *some* capacity for controlling behavior and managing emotions. Their capacity for self-control is often diminished in the presence of too much environmental stimulation. We want to provide them with sufficient structure to experience the same spiritual benefits as other attendees. Again, in part 2, I'll share specific strategies for welcoming children and adults who lack self-control.

As we transition to our next ministry strategy, imagine how you might redesign your church's ministry spaces if every child and adult attending had ADHD. What if everyone in attendance had an untreated anxiety disorder? Or if your church was filled with kids and adults with obsessive-compulsive disorder who go to great lengths to avoid germs? Could you modify your spaces in ways that would improve the experience of everyone in attendance? These are the challenges we face in developing our mental health inclusion strategies.

STRATEGY #3: FOCUS ON ACTIVITIES MOST ESSENTIAL FOR SPIRITUAL GROWTH

Our mission at Key Ministry is to "promote meaningful connection between churches and families of kids with disabilities for the purpose of making disciples of Jesus Christ."[6] The church exists to make disciples. I'm writing this book because I want churches to become more impactful in making disciples among families touched by mental illness. Most churches have lots of methods and strategies for making disciples and a limited pool of time, talent, volunteers, and money to support their efforts. While God *could* choose to grant your church infinite human and financial resources to implement your mental health inclusion strategy, his customary practice is to position churches with more ministry opportunities than resources. If you were to invite me to be part of your planning team and you had limited time and energy to put into the development of a comprehensive ministry strategy, I'd encourage you to focus available resources on increasing participation in the one or two ministry activities and practices that your church has found most effective in advancing spiritual growth.

The leadership of Willow Creek Community Church in suburban Chicago conducted a study about a decade ago of the spiritual practices of congregants from their church, along with two hundred other churches of various sizes and denominational affiliations, to identify the most essential practices for promoting spiritual growth.[7] They identified fifty factors that contribute to spiritual growth and divided them into four categories:

- adoption of core Christian beliefs and attitudes
- involvement in organized church activities (worship services, small groups, adult education, service projects)
- personal spiritual practices (or disciplines)
- spiritual activities with others outside of the organized church

Your church probably places greater emphasis on some church activities and spiritual practices than others. Churches with dynamic and effective teaching pastors may prioritize attendance at worship services and large group studies. Active participation in small groups may be an expectation in others. Some churches heavily encourage member participation in community service or missions. Regardless of the approach your church uses to make disciples, your inclusion team will want to focus attention and resources on welcoming new guests who come as a result of your mental health ministry efforts into the most critical ministry activities and environments and the ones with the greatest impact.

Keep in mind that the activities most critical for spiritual growth may not necessarily take place on Sunday morning. Here are some practical steps churches can implement to involve children, teens, and families in high-impact activities that take place away from the church or outside of scheduled worship times:

If your church's principal strategy for promoting spiritual growth is the teaching offered during weekend worship services, offer to host a special worship and prayer service for families impacted by mental illness in your community, and assign your church's most effective and engaging preacher the task of providing a relevant message during the service.

If small group participation is essential to your discipleship strategy, provide qualified child care to support biological, adoptive, and foster parents in attending small groups.

If your church emphasizes participation in outwardly focused service projects and activities, identify appropriate roles and functions for persons of all abilities in your missional activities and provide alternative methods for volunteers who are shy or less socially adept to communicate their interest in serving.

Help members who struggle to prioritize time for Bible study or other spiritual disciplines by promoting relationships with accountability partners to provide necessary reminders and encouragement.

I'll share additional ideas in part 2 as I lay out a strategy for surmounting challenges to church participation for those with common mental health conditions.

STRATEGY #4: COMMUNICATE EFFECTIVELY

A key step for any church seeking to include those affected by mental illness is to establish a culture that explicitly grants permission for mental health to be a topic of conversation. The words and teaching that emanate from the pulpit and are propagated through a church's online platforms can either perpetuate or eradicate stigma.

A Verbal Communication Strategy

The 2014 LifeWay Research report on the church and mental health I referenced in chapter 1 reported that persons with mental illness and their family members want their churches to openly discuss mental health issues.[8] The statistics lead me to believe that the most powerful way that your church can communicate acceptance of kids and adults with mental health conditions is to preach it from the pulpit.

Perry Noble was remarkably open in sharing his story while serving as pastor of NewSpring Church in Anderson, South Carolina. He is the author of *Overwhelmed*—a book in which he relates his experiences of anxiety and trauma.[9] He addressed what he sees as the church's greatest misperceptions about mental illness in an interview with the *Christian Post*.

> Too many people think that being overwhelmed, dealing with depression and such is only a spiritual issue, and that if a person simply prayed and read their Bible more it would go away. Nothing could be further from the truth. Mental illness is a serious issue that the church must be willing to address with compassion, not condemnation. Typically, we criticize and attack what we do not understand. I believe that if the church were more willing to try to understand the reality of mental illness, many people could be helped.[10]

Other pastors speak from their experiences as parents or family members of someone with mental illness. For example, Rick Warren has preached extensively on mental health-related topics in the aftermath of his son's suicide in 2013.

While it's important for pastors and other church leaders to speak publicly about these issues, understanding *what not to say* from the pulpit or through social media is an equally important communication concern. Amy Simpson is a writer and publishing executive who currently serves as a contributing editor to *Christianity Today*. She has written two books on mental health-related topics and has described ten ways in which mental illness continues to be stigmatized in the church. Communication that pastors and church leaders may want to avoid includes:

- teaching that communicates the message, intentional or not, that Christians don't have serious problems
- teaching that perpetuates misunderstanding and mistrust of psychology
- teaching that suggests that mental illness is God's punishment

- teaching that claims mental illness is evidence of weak faith or flagrant sin
- teaching that proposes purely spiritual solutions to medical problems[11]

Despite our intense preoccupation in Western culture with political correctness, making fun of people with mental health conditions has maintained a degree of acceptability in many circles. I wish it didn't need to be said, but church leaders must avoid using derogatory terms like *crazy*, *insane*, or *psycho* and try to refrain from referring to persons with diagnostic terms descriptive of behavior patterns, using words like *manic*, *hyper*, or *OCD*.

Use of people-first language is just as important when talking about mental health conditions as it is in discussing any other disability. What do I mean by people-first language? We don't *define someone* by their disability or condition when we talk about them. Instead we talk about the issue they struggle with. Note the difference between referring to someone as "my friend with depression" as opposed to "my depressed friend." I encourage pastors and other church leaders to be nuanced in the way they talk about people with mental illness in both public and private communication. I would also add several other suggestions to Amy's list of what *not to say or do* publicly, especially from the pulpit:

- **Don't minimize the severity of mental illness.** People die from mental illness. More Americans between the ages of fifteen and thirty-four will die from suicide this year than by heart disease, cancer, and diabetes combined.[12]
- **Don't question the validity of specific diagnoses.** You have no idea how much research and scientific debate goes into justifying the inclusion of specific conditions in the International Classification of Diseases (ICD-10) and the *Diagnostic and Statistical Manual of Mental Disorders* (*DSM-5*)—the two primary systems used worldwide for categorizing mental illness.

- **Don't question the legitimacy of treatments dispensed by licensed professionals.** Undermining the confidence of your members and attendees in recommendations from professionals with appropriate training and certification may lead to avoidance or refusal of beneficial treatments and intensify or prolong suffering.
- **Don't assume that spiritual remedies alone will be the only way that God chooses to heal persons with mental illness.** If we pray with the presumption that God can use surgeons and physicians and medicine to cure diseases of the body when our friends and loved ones are ill, why assume that God won't use psychiatrists and therapists and medication to heal conditions of the mind?

A Digital Communication Strategy

In addition to sermons and public announcements, email, websites, and social media represent key communication channels for the church in the twenty-first century. Our new digital platforms afford us unique opportunities to reach people no one else is reaching.

Websites increasingly serve as the front door to our churches. Social media platforms have become essential tools for communicating with church attendees and promotion of ministry opportunities and events. From my observations on Sunday morning, far more members of my church stay up-to-date on upcoming events and opportunities through a Thursday email blast to the congregation or the video announcements in the early part of the worship service than through printed bulletins. Glowing smartphones and tablets have largely replaced the rustling of pages in Bibles when the time comes for the morning Scripture reading.

The initial impressions of potential visitors are increasingly a product of your church's internet presence. Your church's digital presence may hold relatively greater importance in connecting with and attracting new visitors impacted by mental illness for a variety of reasons I'll discuss in upcoming chapters. Here are three general concepts pertinent to our target population for churches to consider in evaluating their web presence:

1. **The more persons with mental illness can see, hear, and experience your ministry environments online, the better.** Anxiety disorders are the most common mental health conditions among adults in the United States, and these disorders represent either the most or second most common category of mental health conditions experienced by children and teens.[13] A fundamental difference in brain function observed among persons with anxiety disorders is a propensity to overestimate the degree of danger or risk in unfamiliar environments or situations. Therefore, the more information and preparation they have in advance of a new situation, the greater the likelihood they can overcome fear and take part in the experience.

2. **Use your church's social media platforms to pass along mental health-related links and posts that attendees can share with friends and neighbors with mental health needs.** In a later chapter on overcoming stigma, I'll introduce you to several wonderful ministries and organizations that provide mental health resources and support in a Christian context. Using your social media platforms to share articles and posts from reputable Christian organizations addressing mental health concerns provides an easy way for your people to let their friends and neighbors impacted by mental illness know that they are welcome at your church, and it represents a tool for engaging your members and attendees in your mental health inclusion efforts.

3. **Think about how your church can use online connections to promote offline experiences of Christian community in which participants enjoy worship, study, and fellowship in the physical presence of one another.** There's a reason they call it *social media*. While online community is real community, the value of platforms such as Facebook, Instagram, and LinkedIn is in helping users maintain and leverage relationships. At Key Ministry, we seek to use our online groups to

facilitate introductions and connections so that families impacted by disability can discover a "bricks and mortar" church where they can worship in the physical presence of other Christ followers. I'll share more ideas for using web technology and social media in the chapter on overcoming social isolation.

In summary, your church's website and social media platforms are powerful tools in any mental health inclusion strategy. Be strategic in making the most of them in any plan!

STRATEGY #5: HELP FAMILIES WITH THEIR MOST HEARTFELT NEEDS

"Small things done with great love will change the world." Those words are carved above the entrance to the main campus of Vineyard Cincinnati, a church that does an extraordinary job of sharing the love of Christ with the people of their surrounding community and region. They also represent an important strategy for connecting with people who may be skeptical about Jesus because of past negative experiences with Christians or with church.

If we're called to impact all people inside and outside the church, including those affected by mental illness, we must first get better at meeting the practical needs of families impacted by mental illness that are already connected to the church, without neglecting those in our community who lack a relationship with Jesus and a church community. Our ministry colleague and former teammate Mike Woods frequently reminds us of the importance of "outwardly focused inclusion." Given the social isolation that families of children with mental illness and trauma often experience, we can't wait for them to come to us; we need to be intentional about going to them.

As churches seek to help kids, teens, and adults with mental illness, start by *making intercessory prayer a priority*. Pray regularly for attendees struggling with mental illness. This is a powerful strategy.

Ponder ways that your church's existing ministries whose purpose is to provide care and support can serve persons with mental illness. Let's look at some examples.

Your church probably has a pastor or a care team responsible for hospital and nursing home visitation. Do they ever visit *psychiatric* hospitals? What about group homes where adults with severe, chronic mental illness live with support? Does anyone from your children's or student ministry staff ever visit group homes or residential treatment centers in your area where kids are placed when their treatment needs can't safely be addressed in the home?

Does your church have a ministry that provides meals when a parent or family member is in the hospital or has a serious illness? Would families in your church receive meals if a spouse or a child was admitted to the psychiatric floor of your local hospital as opposed to a medical or pediatric floor? What if a family needed to spend several evenings a week transporting a teen to an intensive outpatient treatment program while they continue to attend school during the day? One measure of success of your mental health initiative will be when families receiving intensive mental health care and support are comfortable informing pastors and church staff of their needs.

Many churches have a deacons' fund or benevolence fund to provide short-term financial assistance to families in need. Would families from your church with no other way of addressing short-term mental health needs be able to access those funds? Gifts from these funds could cover one-time consultations or prescription refills, transportation needs, or child care for adults who care for loved ones in the hospital.

Your church could address a pressing need in your community by making affordable counseling services available. Khesed is a nonprofit organization that uses a model in which churches with vacant or underutilized office space make their space available at no cost to licensed mental health professionals who are willing to provide affordable and rapidly accessible services in underserved communities.[14] Your church could also provide financial assistance for counseling services. Many churches provide counseling services for adults but have little to offer a child or teen. While not an everyday occurrence, our practice has been contacted by churches or Christian schools when families have a need but parents lack sufficient funds or insurance benefits to access quality care from a clinician supportive of the family's beliefs and value system.

Many churches maintain referral lists of mental health professionals for families in need. Is your church's referral list reasonably current? Would your church be willing to go the extra mile to assist families that are bewildered by the process of making appointments for mental health care and accessing insurance benefits?

Is your church involved with a homeless ministry or prison ministry? If you are, you may well be involved with mental health ministry and not even know it! The Substance Abuse and Mental Health Services Administration (SAMHSA) describes one in five homeless persons as having "severe mental illness."[15] Per statistics from the US Department of Justice, approximately, 24 percent of jail inmates, 15 percent of state prisoners, and 10 percent of federal prisoners reported at least one symptom of a psychotic disorder. Local jail inmates had the highest rate of symptoms of a mental health disorder (60 percent), followed by state (49 percent) and federal prisoners (40 percent).[16] Ask yourself how your church can better support the mental health needs of persons you already serve through these ministries.

As you pursue this strategy, these words from Scripture are good to remember:

> What good is it, my brothers and sisters, if someone claims to have faith but has no deeds? Can such faith save them? Suppose a brother or a sister is without clothes and daily food. If one of you says to them, "Go in peace; keep warm and well fed," but does nothing about their physical needs, what good is it? In the same way, faith by itself, if it is not accompanied by action, is dead.
>
> *James 2:14–17*

STRATEGY #6: OFFER EDUCATION AND SUPPORT

For churches that place high value on community and encourage small group ministry involvement, establishing groups to help address the unique support needs of individuals and families is a great starting place for a mental health inclusion strategy. The availability of *education and support groups* sends a powerful message to church members and the surrounding community that persons affected by mental illness and their families will be warmly welcomed. Plus, offering groups introduces to your church people who would never otherwise attend a weekend worship service and helps promote relationships between church members and persons outside of the church. Groups also represent a practical and inexpensive strategy for meeting the heartfelt needs of marginalized people in the community your church serves.

For many churches, the decision to initiate a mental health inclusion strategy is the direct result of pastors, church leaders, and key volunteers seeking to become better educated about the needs of persons with mental illness. For leaders and ministry teams looking to learn more, Joe Padilla and his team at the Mental Health Grace Alliance are a great resource.[17] The Grace Alliance is a Christian mental health recovery and support organization that provides resources, support groups, and training to pastors and community leaders so they can help those affected by mental illness. They offer several types of church-based education and support groups. In a 2015 article Joe wrote for Key Ministry, he emphasized the importance of curriculum-focused support as opposed to "share groups" without a defined structure:

> Share groups focus on relational conversations and do not follow a structure. The good news is that these groups build strong relationships . . . the bad news is they turn into discouraging venting groups. Research reveals these groups are not effective; they focus on co-rumination over problems that reinforce aggression,

maladaptive thoughts, depression and anxiety. Groups that follow a curriculum or guide have more effective results with relationships and personal growth (health).[18]

Several models of mental health education and support groups are currently in place in a large number of churches. Contact information for each sponsoring organization is kept current on Key Ministry's website (www.keyministry.org).

NAMI Groups

The National Alliance on Mental Illness (NAMI) offers two types of classes that I highly recommend. The first is NAMI Family-to-Family, which is a twelve-session educational program for family, significant others, and friends of people living with mental illness.[19] Family-to-Family has been shown to significantly improve coping and problem-solving abilities of the people closest to persons with mental health disorders. Each class is led by family members trained by NAMI to follow a set curriculum that uses presentations, discussion questions, and interactive exercises. They also offer NAMI Basics for parents and caregivers of children and teens with mental illness—a six-session course with a similar design to Family-to-Family.[20] NAMI also sponsors an initiative (NAMI FaithNet) for networking members with mental health advocates, clergy, and congregations of all faith traditions.[21]

Fresh Hope

Fresh Hope is a Christian-based peer-support recovery model developed by Brad Hoefs, a Lutheran pastor with a twenty-year history of bipolar disorder associated with extended periods of depression.[22] Fresh Hope groups are organized around six tenets; include family members and caregivers, along with individuals with mental health conditions; and are focused on specifics topics related to the medical, physical, social, emotional, and spiritual components of recovery.

Grace Groups

Grace Groups are offered through Mental Health Grace Alliance and provide psychoeducational materials, skills, and tools to improve mental health wellness and recovery.[23] Mental Health Grace Alliance has developed Christ-centered, curriculum-based models for family and peer support groups, trauma and PTSD groups, and young adult groups. The material is designed to work within any denomination, and published research demonstrates the benefits of these groups.[24]

■ ■ ■

If your church already offers some type of mental health education or support group, I encourage you to consider taking a next step by developing a strategy to include individuals and families served by your groups into the full range of ministry activities and experiences offered through your church.

STRATEGY #7: GIVE YOUR PEOPLE RESPONSIBILITY FOR MINISTRY

Your church will never fulfill the promise of your mental health inclusion ministry unless the people in your church experience the privilege of *doing* ministry and are given the opportunity to own their roles in the ministry. The people who attend your church are your greatest assets in reaching and building relationships with persons in your community affected by mental illness who have yet to come to faith in Jesus. Given the statistics I shared earlier about how common mental illness is in the United States, it's fair to assume that most kids and adults who come to your church will know at least one person with mental illness who lacks a meaningful connection to a local church. Empowering your people to become the hands and feet of Jesus is a key to expanding your impact.

I was lamenting the American church's apparent lack of impact on the larger culture over breakfast with a pastor friend while writing this chapter. My lament led into a discussion of the roles and responsibilities of church staff. The pastor friend believed the most essential role his staff could play was to come alongside church members doing ministry with resources and support. Through this approach, staff could greatly expand their influence beyond the work they were able to complete, while making their lives a great deal easier.

There are several ways for a mental health inclusion team to facilitate a ministry owned by the people of your church. One method is by *celebrating and encouraging acts of service.* Sharing stories of how your people reached out to and built relationships with persons affected by mental illness and detailing the ways God is at work through those relationships are great strategies for inspiring others to serve and to model how they can "be the church" to those without a church.

The most meaningful ministry a church can offer typically occurs through the spontaneous action of individual Christians who recognize and respond to needs right where God has placed them. Libby Peterson, who leads the family ministry at my church, offers several practical suggestions for casting a vision for ministry:

> Begin to seek God's help in building a relationship. Invite the mom for coffee, the dad to a sporting event, the child for a play date, offer to grab groceries on your next trip or just call some afternoon to say "Hi." Trust the Lord will use that relationship for HIS glory—after all Jesus lives IN YOU and as this family grows in relationship with you—they will inevitably begin to see Jesus. Watch for opportunities to BRING them into a gathering of people who love Jesus. Be open to inviting them to belong— and know that it's in the belonging that people often first come to believe![25]

Other members and attendees may have more defined roles— serving on your inclusion team, leading a small group, providing respite care, or helping to publicize the ministry. Everyone in your church has gifts and talents to contribute to this ministry.

You can empower your people through resourcing them for evangelism. Every believer in your church can share the good news with those whom God places in their path. How can your inclusion team keep mental health inclusion at the forefront of their minds? During our discussion of communication strategies, we touched on the importance of making resources readily available through social media. Given that the average American adult now spends more than ten hours *each day* consuming electronic media, your members and attendees are increasingly likely to encounter people whom God places along their *digital* path.[26] Consider what your team can do to provide them with tools for inviting online friends with mental illness to your church.

Your people provide an invaluable witness through offering the ministry of presence. In a culture of service and action, it's important to hear this word of mere presence as ministry. I like how Luke Monahan and Caroline Renehan describe the ministry of presence as "a faith presence [that] accompanies each person on the journey through life."[27] Mary Glenn of the Fuller Youth Institute elaborates on the ministry of presence:

> This presence in each of us reflects God's presence, love, and peace. Central to this ministry philosophy is the idea of "**being with**." The love and presence of God is embodied as we are *with* the other person in their moment of crisis.
>
> A ministry of presence can bring comfort and express care without words. Presence encompasses physical, emotional, and spiritual care. **This is sacramental presence.** It is a revelation of Jesus' care and compassion through listening, being with, and affirming.[28]

In our increasingly frantic culture, is there a more generous way to affirm the value of every person as an image bearer of God than by simply being present for them?

Your church is everywhere your people are. How will your team resource and support them, wherever God has placed them, so they can do the work of ministry with children, teens, and adults who experience the effects of mental illness?

I've identified seven barriers to church participation of those who struggle with mental illness, as well as an array of ministry strategies that form the foundation of a mental health inclusion initiative. In part 2, I'll share lots of practical ideas for reaching out and welcoming new friends who have been missing for far too long.

PART 2

A MENTAL HEALTH INCLUSION STRATEGY

SIX

Overcoming Stigma in the Church

Some churches actually intentionally reject people with mental illness. In their theological framework, mental illness has no place among God's people . . . But most churches do not hold to the kind of theology that overtly blames, rejects, and casts out people whose brains have shown themselves particularly vulnerable to the forces of disease and decay that haunt us all in various ways. Even so, many inadvertently communicate rejection through their policies or culture.

AMY SIMPSON, AUTHOR OF *TROUBLED MINDS*

I'm becoming more and more encouraged by the progress being made in both the broader culture and church culture in eliminating the stigma associated with mental illness. The rapid proliferation of research demonstrating the biological basis of mental illness made possible by advances in brain imaging and genetics and our growing understanding of the mechanisms through which environmental influences impact brain development and genetic expression are changing attitudes and opinions inside and outside of the church. The willingness of prominent Christians to publicly discuss their personal or family experiences of mental illness has been extremely helpful in reducing stigma within the church. When Rick Warren proclaims, "It's not a sin to be sick" on Facebook, church leaders who respect his teaching and ministry are more inclined to rethink their assumptions about mental health.[1]

The church has often struggled to separate its antipathy for the ideas embraced by thought leaders in psychiatry and psychology from people who turn to mental health professionals in search of help. I want men, women, and children affected by mental illness to fully benefit from churches that proclaim the truth contained in Scripture as it has been accepted and understood by pastors, church leaders, and students of the Bible for nearly two thousand years. As someone who was raised in the Catholic faith, served in leadership as an adult in churches rooted in Arminian and Reformed theology, and spent considerable time studying the Bible, I am not aware of a theological principle or Scripture compromised by any scientific finding to date related to mental illness or intentional ministry to persons with mental illness. I think the apostle Paul describes nicely in Ephesians 4:11–15 the essence of what we seek to do in our mental health inclusion strategy, namely, build up the body of Christ in sound doctrine through sharing the truth in love.

With that said, the LifeWay study I referenced earlier that reported that more than 50 percent of adults who don't attend church see us as unwelcoming to persons with mental illness provides evidence that perceptions change slowly. We need to tackle our image problem when it comes to mental illness to earn the privilege of sharing the gospel with those who are outside the church.

The good news is that your church takes a huge step in eliminating stigma when it publicly acknowledges any intentional effort to welcome and include persons with mental illness. In this chapter, we'll look at steps your inclusion team can take to eradicate any existing stigma within your church and to help change attitudes and perceptions in your community about the church and mental illness.

THE MOST IMPORTANT STRATEGIES FOR OVERCOMING STIGMA

Looking back on the seven inclusion strategies introduced in chapter 5, the most important strategies for overcoming stigma include developing and executing a communication plan for mental health-related issues, offering mental health education and support programs providing practical care and support to individuals and families impacted by mental illness both within your church and in your surrounding community, and mobilizing your people to spread the word about your resources within their social networks and circles of influence. The composition of your inclusion team itself may represent an intentional strategy for influencing perceptions of stigma both inside and outside your church.

Communication: It's OK to Talk about Mental Illness

When leaders talk about mental illness during weekend worship services, they communicate to the church body that people with mental illness are valued and grant permission for members and attendees to talk about it. If mental health inclusion is important at your church, you'll want to urge your pastoral team to talk about it on Sunday mornings. Finding a pastor with personal experience to preach on mental illness shouldn't be too difficult: 23 percent of pastors surveyed in the LifeWay study reported they had struggled personally with mental illness.[2]

Another communication strategy is to encourage spiritually mature members and attendees impacted by mental health concerns to share their stories of how God has used their experiences to deepen their faith or influence their spiritual growth (with their permission, of course). Members may be more comfortable sharing their stories via prerecorded video in churches that use video resources in their worship services. Video affords the opportunity for members to rerecord their stories if they leave out important thoughts or details, minimizes the performance anxiety that affects many people when speaking in front of a large group, and is readily shared with friends and acquaintances who might draw encouragement from the stories. As your mental health inclusion initiative begins to bear fruit, stories from persons who have been drawn to your church because of your ministry are especially powerful!

Not every pastor or teacher will have a personal experience of mental illness to share, but every pastor or teacher can find opportunities to demonstrate empathy for the struggles endured by many in your congregation. Many will draw comfort and support from a pastor's willingness to acknowledge their pain and discomfort. A pastor preaching a message on hope can acknowledge that the topic is very likely more difficult for someone experiencing hopelessness as a symptom of depression, or point out in a message on fear that persons with great faith often still experience anxiety on this side of heaven because of their human nature.

In a church where mental health concerns are openly discussed from the pulpit, members and attendees are more likely to be forthcoming about their own mental health challenges and more comfortable in speaking with church staff, small group leaders, and volunteers when they or a family member experience issues that affect their church experience.

Churches have other tools beyond the spoken word in weekend worship services to communicate their willingness to minister with persons with mental health problems. One decidedly low-tech method is the church bulletin. If your church is intentional in providing mental health education or support or offering services of special interest to individuals and families impacted by mental illness, would a first-time visitor to your church know about those resources and services from looking at your bulletin? If a church member or guest knew someone who could benefit from your resources or supports and shared your church's bulletin with them, would that person have enough information to easily access what they want or need?

The same principle holds true for online resources. In the last chapter, we saw how websites increasingly represent the initial point of contact between churches and potential guests. One way to send a clear signal to your local community that persons with mental health conditions are welcome at your church is to ensure that a first-time visitor to your church's website can quickly discover the steps your church is taking to care for and support individuals and families impacted by mental illness.

Mental Health Education and Support

If there is no one in your church or on your inclusion team who can help educate senior leadership on mental health-related issues, one place to begin is by accessing the "Mental Health 101" for church and community leaders course through Mental Health Grace Alliance.[3] The four-hour-long course is designed to help leaders recognize the differences between mental health disorders and emotional issues, to learn how to most appropriately respond to persons with mental health difficulties and their families, to build partnerships with the professional community for helping church members and attendees to access necessary services, and to build simple and supportive pastoral care and community supports.

Your church may want to consider serving as a host site for this course and making it available to other churches in your region. If you do, asking local advocacy groups (such as your local NAMI chapter or mental health board), treatment facilities, schools, and mental health professionals to help promote the event is a great way to enhance the reputation of your church within your local mental health community.

In the previous chapter, you were introduced to several models of mental health education and support from both Christian and secular organizations. In addition to the direct benefits participants gain from these groups, congregations that host and promote such groups are effectively putting out a welcome mat to families in their surrounding communities affected by mental illness. Through offering and promoting support and education groups, your inclusion team diffuses stigma and creates a positive association between your church and a mental health-specific service among potential visitors.

A subtle, yet powerful method for eliminating stigma within the church is to explicitly state the desire of your church's pastoral care team to respond to mental health or family crises.

In the last chapter, I noted that families often miss out on the care and support routinely offered to other families when a member is experiencing a mental health crisis—mentioning, for example, that families are often overlooked by ministries that supply prepared meals when a family member or caregiver is hospitalized. Consider how your website or printed materials could encourage church members to notify the pastoral care team when families are experiencing mental health-related needs, including hospital visitation and support with meals, child care, or transportation.

At the same time we address mental health stigma in the church, we must recognize that stigma is still a significant problem in our broader society. Church members and attendees have valid reasons for protecting the privacy of information regarding mental health diagnoses and treatment. Policies and procedures for ensuring the confidentiality of mental health-related information, including the nature of any special accommodations provided at school or in the workplace, should be developed and clearly communicated to church staff and volunteers. While it's important for your members to know that a pastor or member of a pastoral care team will come to visit them if they are admitted to a psychiatric hospital, they also need to know that if your church publishes a weekly listing of members in hospitals, rehabilitation facilities, and nursing homes, no information will be shared in the church bulletin without their permission.

Mobilizing Your People to Spread the Word

Every member, attendee, and visitor to your church represents a resource for extending your mental health inclusion efforts. Two ways in which your members can be specifically engaged in efforts to eradicate mental health stigma involve using their smartphones, tablets, computers, and social media platforms to function as an extension of your church's communication team and supplying volunteers to organizations that provide mental health resources and support.

Your church probably has a Facebook page or Twitter account. One way for your church's communication team to signal your receptiveness to families impacted by mental illness is to regularly share helpful stories, resources, articles, and links through your social media platforms and encourage your followers to share your resources through their personal accounts. Every share of a mental health-related story originating from your church is free advertising for your church's inclusion strategy and influences the perception of your church among nonbelievers. If your social media team needs good content to share, I suggest following the social media accounts of Key Ministry and those of the other ministries, authors, and influential Christians mentioned throughout this book.

Another way to reduce stigma while building relationships within your mental health community is to assemble volunteer teams to serve local advocacy organizations or treatment facilities. Your church could organize and promote a team to participate in the fund-raising walks sponsored by your local chapter of the National Alliance on Mental Illness (NAMI). NAMI Walks represent the primary mechanism through which local chapters raise the funds they need to support their education programs, support groups, and advocacy efforts.

Many churches mobilize volunteers for community service days. Your inclusion team could select a nonprofit agency that provides mental health services the next time your church plans a service event. Most publicly funded mental health clinics operate on very tight budgets and have little money to pay for landscaping and facility upkeep. Your community likely has one or more agencies that provide housing for adults with severe mental illness. Volunteer teams with experience in home maintenance and repair can help ensure their housing is pleasant and attractive.

BUILDING YOUR INCLUSION TEAM

The decisions made in putting together your inclusion team may take into consideration their potential impact on perceptions of stigma, both in your church and the surrounding community.

Is there anyone on your inclusion team who is known by fellow church members to have a mental illness? Demonstrating that persons with mental illness have gifts and talents of value through empowering them to serve the church in important ministry roles, including participation on your inclusion team, is one strategy for combating stigma in your church.

Another strategy that can impact community perceptions of stigma in the church is to recruit someone from outside your church who has a platform in the mental health community to be a member of your team or a consultant. You may consider inviting the executive director or a senior staff member from your local mental health board, or a senior leader from a prominent mental health organization. Another option may be someone involved in leadership with a local mental health advocacy group, such as NAMI.

A good inclusion plan can result in your church developing a reputation for being stigma *busters* rather than stigma *builders*. I trust that your inclusion team will make use of these ideas—and generate some of your own—to counter the perception that churches represent hostile territory for persons with mental illness and their families.

SEVEN

Overcoming Anxiety

Do not be anxious about anything, but in every situation, by prayer and petition, with thanksgiving, present your requests to God. And the peace of God, which transcends all understanding, will guard your hearts and your minds in Christ Jesus.

PHILIPPIANS 4:6–7

David Zimmerman is a former pastor who now helps churches market themselves to new visitors. He claims that the most pressing concern for a first-time church visitor is that they make sure to do nothing to embarrass themselves during the service.[1] His observation is especially relevant for a child or an adult who has an anxiety disorder.

A follower of our ministry's Facebook page shared this vignette in response to an article from Focus on the Family titled "Is Your Church Unnecessarily Uncomfortable?"[2]

> One Christmas Eve, we attended a different church because ours did not have a service that year, and we still wanted to go to one. What we found was not a "typical" Christmas Eve service but one in which they went around to every person sitting in the

room and asked them to stand up and share a personal story of how God had worked in their life during that year along with a hymn request that matched their story. We were expected to do this too, and since we knew no one in the room, it was definitely a little awkward.

Also, we were "pounced on" by so many people welcoming us and inviting us to some upcoming event or Sunday school class that we finally started having to let people know that we were regular attenders and members at another church and likely wouldn't be coming back. We felt really rude saying it, but we had to just to get out the door without having to get involved in ten different conversations. My husband was on staff at the time at our home church and helped oversee our "first impressions" area. Boy, did we learn about what NOT to do that evening!

WHAT STRATEGIES ARE MOST IMPORTANT FOR OVERCOMING ANXIETY?

Children or adults with anxiety are likely to experience distress from the demands of the assimilation process necessary for entering your ministry environments. I'll take a closer look at those processes and identify potential sources of embarrassment for both visitors and long-standing attendees in your most impactful church programming. I'll examine the role your church's web platforms and electronic communication systems play in enhancing engagement among guests and members with anxiety, as well as touch on the importance of staff and volunteer training and education. I'll conclude by discussing ways that members and regular attendees can help their friends and neighbors with anxiety to have better experiences of church.

Visiting Church in Their Shoes

To better understand the types of challenges a family affected by common anxiety disorders may experience in visiting a church for the first time or establishing a regular pattern of involvement at church, allow me to introduce you to the Petersons. They're typical of the families I see in my practice and represent the type of folks who are often targeted by churches in their evangelism and outreach strategies.

Michael and Jessica Peterson have been married for thirteen years. They have a ten-year-old son (Jacob) and a seven-year-old daughter (Emily). Jacob was invited by a friend to attend Vacation Bible School at a church near their home. He had a great time and is badgering his parents to bring him to church every Sunday.

Jessica attended church regularly in her youth and has wanted her children to have the same experience she did, but her husband had little interest in going, and the very thought of visiting different churches felt overwhelming because of her social anxiety and agoraphobia. She almost always experiences anxiety around unfamiliar people and fears others will judge her negatively if they see her hands begin to shake or if she struggles to make small talk. Whenever possible, she avoids speaking with anyone outside of her immediate family and one or two longtime friends, either in person or by phone. When she and her husband go out, they avoid crowded restaurants and wait several weeks to see popular movies so she can have an aisle seat in a sparsely attended theater.

Jessica's daughter has been diagnosed with separation anxiety disorder. Emily often becomes tearful and irritable on Sunday evenings in anticipation of going to school on Monday, turns up in the nurse's office on a weekly basis with stomachaches, and is prone to tantrums if she wakes up at night and is locked out of her parents' bedroom. Michael's work responsibilities cause him to be unavailable on Sundays.

If Jessica accedes to Jacob's request and agrees to take him and his sister to church on Sunday, consider all the challenges their family could experience in attending a weekend worship service. Between arriving and exiting the church parking lot, Jessica will:

- worry that either she or her children will draw the attention of others for being dressed inappropriately.

- encounter one or two greeters on her way into the building.
- need directions to the children's ministry area.
- need to speak with at least one staff member or volunteer to register her kids for children's ministry.
- meet the ministry volunteer responsible for each of her children's breakout groups and possibly the children's ministry director.
- need to respond to Emily's emotional reaction when she learns she's expected to go to a worship service and Sunday school for kids her age in an area of the church away from her mom. Jessica will worry what others will think if Emily is the only child in the worship service for adults.
- encounter an usher at the entrance to the worship center.
- scan the worship center for available seats on an aisle near an exit. *What if those seats are taken?*
- need to interact with attendees seated nearby, especially if the church has a designated "meet and greet" time.
- be asked to complete an information card requesting her name, address, phone number, and email and spend the remainder of the service fearing the prospect of a phone call or visit from the church.

During the service, Jessica discovers that attendees are encouraged to join a small group with four or five other couples for Bible studies or book discussions. She may be reminded to stop at the visitors' center following the service, where another team of volunteers has a small gift for her. In a small church, she may meet the pastor as she exits the worship center. She'll repeat the process she went through before the service began in retrieving her kids from the children's ministry area. For good measure, she may encounter one or two additional greeters as her family leaves for the parking lot.

This process is typical for a first-time visitor at many churches in North America. Imagine how you might feel after a morning at church if the prospect of interacting with unfamiliar people caused you intense fear. One in fifteen adults in the United States are affected with the type of anxiety Jessica experiences.

How could someone like Jessica be made more comfortable during an initial church visit? What could an easier process look like?

Let's go a step further and assume that Jessica navigates the gauntlet of social interactions during her family's initial visit and the level of discomfort she and Emily experience is somewhat manageable. How could the church support her in joining a small group? How could she and her family serve in the church? What challenges might she experience if she wishes to become a member? Will she need to make a profession of faith or offer a public testimony as a condition for baptism or membership?

Catherine Boyle of Outside In Ministries recommends that churches identify a *mental health liaison*—a primary contact person for church members and visitors who might require assistance before or during an initial visit or benefit from accommodations in church activities they find challenging.[3] Persons with anxiety may experience less frustration and distress in navigating church systems through interacting by phone, email, or text with one sympathetic staff member or volunteer who functions as an advocate.

I'd compare the benefits of a mental health liaison to those of an airport club membership. When I was a frequent flyer, cancellations or delays had the potential to wreak havoc on my "doctor" and "dad" commitments. I found that the front desk staff at the airport club could quickly bypass any obstacle preventing me from getting home quickly. My President's Club membership with Continental Airlines was worth every penny I paid for it!

Imagine if Jessica discovered that there was someone she could contact electronically while checking out the church's website who could help pave the way for a successful initial visit. The liaison might work with church staff members who are responsible for welcoming and assimilating visitors and families like Jessica's in any number of ways.

When kids with anxiety are faced with the prospect of attending a new school, we don't throw them to the wolves on the first day. Instead, *we prepare them for the experience.* A key support element in any transition is allowing them to become familiar with their new environment when only a few people are watching. When a football team plays a road game, they often head directly to the opposing team's stadium for a walk-through after getting off the team plane or bus. This is an informal practice conducted without pads to help players become acclimated to their new surroundings before facing a loud and boisterous crowd on game day. A liaison can offer persons with anxiety (or parents of a child with anxiety) an opportunity for a walk-through prior to attending church on a weekend.

When children who struggle with transitions or unfamiliar situations are prepared for their first day in a new grade or a new school, they're given the opportunity to meet their teachers, find their locker, locate their classrooms, visit areas of the school where special classes (art, music) take place, and see where they will be changing clothes for gym class. A church walk-through could include showing kids and parents where they'll enter church and check in for their age-appropriate ministry and visiting the spaces for large group worship or teaching and breakout activities in smaller groups. Kids will see where their parents will be while they're engaged in age-appropriate ministry activities. Even if teachers or group leaders aren't available to do a walk-through during the week, a liaison with a smartphone can prerecord video introductions for use in a visit.

When families of kids with anxiety vent their frustrations with church in my office, their most common complaint involves arbitrary rules or decisions that cause their child to be separated from someone they depend on for companionship. Their child might be more comfortable with a peer or sibling in a Sunday school class a year ahead of or a year behind their grade placement in school, but the children's or student ministry teams are reluctant to establish a precedent by making exceptions to their practices. A liaison can work with staff and volunteers in negotiating appropriate accommodations.

Many teens from our practice commit to retreats or mission trips but drop out at the last minute if they can't share a room or cabin with a familiar friend. A liaison can serve as an intermediary between families and the staff or volunteers responsible for the trips to work out satisfactory housing arrangements.

If small group participation is an essential component of your church's spiritual growth strategy, how could you make the process of *finding a group* and the experience of *belonging to a group* more comfortable for children, teens, and adults with anxiety who may have great trepidation at the expectation for self-disclosure?

Consider how your church's members and attendees find groups to join. Some churches hold large social events for individuals or couples to find groups close to where they live or work with others of similar interests. What if a large, public "meet and greet" event is too intimidating or evokes memories of having been the last person picked for the kickball team at recess in grade school? Could your church maintain an *alternative path to connecting with groups* for those who find the process overwhelming?

Your inclusion team could work with your church's small group ministry to identify groups whose composition or leadership is better suited to persons with anxiety or any other mental health condition. A liaison from your team could help facilitate introductions between persons with anxiety and appropriate small group leaders. They may also help persons with anxiety leave groups if group participation becomes too overwhelming. I've had many people with anxiety describe how they'll search for the nearest exit immediately after boarding a plane, checking into a hotel room, or being seated in a restaurant. They need to know a way out if they feel unsafe. Persons with anxiety won't join groups if they're not sure there's a way to leave if they need to.

Welcoming Ministry Environments for Persons with Anxiety

Many children and adults are vulnerable to more intense symptoms of anxiety in the presence of large crowds. Their awareness of becoming visibly anxious in the presence of others leads to more anxiety. They may be especially vulnerable near busy entrances and exits and check-in areas where children separate from parents. Children and adults prone to this type of cascading anxiety may benefit from having a quiet space with a measure of privacy where they can gather their emotions if they experience overwhelming distress, if such space is available at your church. Members of your church's team who are responsible for welcoming guests (ushers, greeters, staff, and volunteers responsible for registration areas) may be made aware of the quiet space and trained to contact select staff members or volunteers trained to accompany children or adults in distress to the space. Spaces close to high traffic areas but out of sight of most attendees work best.

Persons with agoraphobia often experience marked fear or anxiety when they're on public transportation, in open spaces, in enclosed places, in crowds, or standing in lines. They avoid these situations because they fear escape may be impossible or help unavailable in the event of panic-like symptoms (pounding, racing heartbeat, acute shortness of breath, overwhelming sense of dread) or that they may be unable to leave without drawing attention to themselves. The worst conceivable seat in church for someone with agoraphobia is a middle seat in a row near the front because *the mere thought* of having to ask others to get up or the awareness that most people in the church will notice their departure may be enough to trigger an anxiety attack.

One inclusion strategy for persons with agoraphobia is for ushers to intentionally reserve seats for persons with anxiety at the ends of rows and near exits. Your church will need to provide guests a method of signaling their need for the seats that enables them to avoid becoming a focus of attention. In a church where attendees wear name tags, the inclusion team could provide these guests with tags that have a different color border (or the name written in a different color of ink) easily recognized by ushers. An alternative method for discreetly indicating a need for preferential seating is to provide guests and regular attendees with Bible covers of a distinctive style or color known to the ushers.

More and more churches that live stream their worship services strategically place television monitors and comfortable seating outside the worship center. This affords guests with anxiety (as well as persons with sensory processing differences) who may be reluctant to self-identify an option for attending services in the event they experience distress while sitting in a large crowd.

A Role for Your Church's Communication Team

We've observed that new visitors and attendees are afraid of embarrassing themselves at church and that persons with anxiety are predisposed to overestimating risk in new situations. We've also noted that churches can help ease anxiety through sharing lots of pictures and videos on websites and social media platforms to help prospective visitors know exactly what they can expect at a weekend worship service. Why not use a similar strategy to help prepare regular attendees and visitors for any of your church's ministry activities?

How helpful could an extensive online photo or video album be for parents or ministry leaders seeking to persuade an anxious child or teen to participate in a special event? A family of a child I treat for anxiety regularly attends a satellite campus of a large, multisite church. Their child has no difficulty at weekend worship events because the campus their family attends is relatively small. Their church hosts a combined Vacation Bible School for all their sites at their main campus that draws more than a thousand kids each summer. My patient turned and ran from his mother directly back to the family's car after his first glimpse of VBS at the main campus. Lots of video and pictures would have helped the parents better prepare their child for the experience.

The same principles hold true with adults. If you have someone in your church who has overcome anxiety to join a small group, participate in a mission trip, or serve in a community outreach activity who is comfortable speaking of their experiences, consider interviewing them for online videos that promote your church's key ministry activities.

Communication is a two-way street. In addition to recognizing the need that our guests and fellow church members with anxiety have for information before new experiences and activities, we must also create alternatives for persons uncomfortable with our channels for communicating information to pastors, church staff, and volunteers. I encourage churches to provide an electronic communication option for every interaction that currently requires a phone call. Using a telephone is very difficult for children and adults who have a variety of anxiety disorders.

Several years ago, our practice was involved in a research study of kids with social anxiety. One of the teens who qualified for the study sent *thirteen thousand text messages in the preceding month without using a single minute of talk time*! The discomfort involved in using a phone may prevent many of your people from participating in activities or events they may otherwise have attended. Our ministry uses an online registration system hosted by Formstack (www.formstack. com) to access any ministry resource or service or to register for any Key Ministry event.

YOUR PEOPLE'S RESPONSIBILITY FOR MINISTRY

Your church's members and attendees are your greatest ministry resource for connecting with individuals and families impacted by anxiety. Encourage them to invite family members, neighbors, and coworkers who are quiet or withdrawn to church activities. Most children and adults will be able to participate in most church activities in the company of one or more trusted companions. This is a great way to release your church into ministry.

Pastors could discuss the signs and symptoms of anxiety in the context of a sermon or a worship service. They could encourage attendees to consider whether anxiety might be a contributing factor among friends or family members who aren't attending church and challenge them to invite someone affected with anxiety by a specific date. The best possible inclusion strategy for persons with anxiety is *the presence of a trusted friend at church.*

For children and adults with anxiety, going into large group situations surrounded by people engaged in conversation with one another truly represents the space between a rock and a hard place. The thought of engaging a relative stranger in conversation is intensely distressing, but the fear of standing out because of being alone is worse. When a friend accompanies someone with anxiety to church, the friend can initiate required social interactions and help them to blend more easily into the crowd. The following story illustrates the importance of companionship at church for someone with anxiety.

I know a teen (Sarah) who was one of the most prized volunteers on her church's children's ministry team. She volunteered during her church's first worship hour on Sundays and attended a teen service during the second hour. One Sunday, the first service ran late, and because Sarah needed to stay in her class until all her kids were picked up, she was late for the teen service. She quietly slipped into a back row by herself. The well-meaning youth pastor saw her from the stage, pointed out that she was sitting alone, and paused so other kids could get up to sit near her.

The following Sunday, Sarah's mother went looking for her between services to discuss transportation arrangements and found her in tears, hiding in a corner, furiously typing on her cell phone. Sarah was desperately texting her friends to find someone who could accompany her to the teen service. Her embarrassment at having been singled out in front of her peers for sitting alone was so great that she never again went to worship alone in that church.

As this chapter on anxiety concludes, let me leave you with one last thought that motivates me to do all I can to help my church welcome our friends and neighbors with anxiety.

Rhett Smith is a pastor and counselor who argues that one of God's purposes in allowing his children to experience anxiety is so they'll increase their dependency on him. He encapsulates this view in his book *The Anxious Christian*.[4] In a guest interview with Key Ministry, Rhett told me, "We are all anxious. We all will and do experience anxiety. Anxiety is part of our human condition. With that being said, I believe that God uses our anxiety as a tool to help us grow. It's a catalyst that keeps us from getting stuck, as it propels us to continually follow God."[5]

What if God is waiting to use our anxiety and the anxiety of our friends and neighbors as an instrument of his glory? How unimaginably sad it would be if a trait that God intended for drawing us into closer relationship with him stood in the way of those who might encounter him through a local church.

EIGHT

Overcoming Executive Functioning Weaknesses

My dear brothers and sisters, take note of this: Everyone should be quick to listen, slow to speak and slow to become angry, because human anger does not produce the righteousness that God desires . . .

Those who consider themselves religious and yet do not keep a tight rein on their tongues deceive themselves, and their religion is worthless.

JAMES 1:19–20, 26

Every culture has customs, values, and behaviors that are often accepted without question by those who belong to that culture. These values and behaviors embody the fundamental values of the group. And it's no different in the church.

All churches have certain cultural customs that reflect what they value, and there are accepted norms of behavior. Expectations can vary greatly between denominations, ethnic groups, and cultural expressions of the church. There are even differences between churches in the same denomination with a similar cultural and ethnic makeup due to the unique history of each congregation. But one constant is that every church has *unwritten* expectations for personal conduct and behavior.

If you don't believe me, try attending a worship service sometime in a church of a different theological persuasion or, better yet, in a different country. In one church, silence may be expected during sermons. Adults quickly grow upset if they hear a child crying and quickly wonder why the mother doesn't leave. But attend a three-hour service in Africa, and you may encounter children running around and several women preparing lunch while the message is shared. Behavior viewed as offensive in one culture is entirely normal in another.

Some churches have very high expectations of their people when it comes to self-discipline and self-control. We often measure the depth of someone's faith and spiritual maturity by their ability to adhere to certain routine practices or spiritual disciplines. Doesn't every good Christian get up before dawn to read their Bible and pray? Doesn't every good Christian set aside time each week to be part of a small group with other men, women, or families?

Our expectations for behavior have lots of support in Scripture. The verses from James at the beginning of the chapter just begin to scratch the surface! Self-control represents one aspect of the fruit of the Spirit listed by Paul in Galatians 5:22–23. James 3 addresses the great importance of controlling our speech. Church leaders are expected to not only demonstrate self-control, but also to cultivate that capacity in their children (1 Timothy 3:2–5).

Clearly, the Bible places a high value on self-control. Being able to control one's behavior and words is evidence of God's work within us. But there is a dark side to using self-control as a key marker in determining spiritual maturity.

What happens when someone with a mental health condition that diminishes their capacity for managing their emotions or behavior wants to attend worship services or participate in other church activities? How should we respond when guests struggle to meet the expectations of our church culture for self-discipline and emotional control because of a *hidden disability* we're not aware of? This question represents a key fault line in the church's understanding of disability and may be the most important explanation for our lack of progress in mental health inclusion ministry.

A highly respected pastor and scholar in the evangelical world led a church with a wonderful disability ministry. Ask yourself if the pastor would have used these words to describe any child served by their special needs ministry:

> A respectful and mannerly 5-year-old unbeliever is better for the world than a more authentic defiant, disrespectful, ill-mannered, unbelieving bully. The family, the friendships, the church, and the world in general will be thankful for parents that restrain the egocentric impulses of their children and confirm in them every impulse toward courtesy and kindness and respect.[1]

The dark side of our attitudes about mental illness comes into full display when we shame and embarrass the very people who should be turning to the church for help. A fascinating study suggested that executive functioning may represent the means through which faith enhances our capacity for self-control.

Researchers had adult volunteers unscramble a series of sentences that included words referring to concepts or themes from the Bible; they were then asked to complete a series of neuropsychological tests that measure executive functions responsible for self-control. The experience of hearing words that enhanced subconscious awareness of God resulted in significantly improved executive functioning. The findings held true even for the one-third of study participants who identified as atheist or agnostic.[2]

Let's take a closer look at how we can address the challenges involved with belonging to a church for children and adults who have

executive functioning deficits. I'll refer specifically to ADHD throughout this chapter, since poor executive functioning is an essential feature
of ADHD, but the inclusion strategies will generally apply to impaired
executive functioning associated with other mental and developmental
disorders—mood disorders, anxiety disorders, psychotic disorders, and
autism spectrum disorders.

WHAT STRATEGIES ARE MOST ESSENTIAL FOR OVERCOMING EXECUTIVE FUNCTIONING DEFICITS?

When it comes to the seven barriers to church participation, children's
and student ministry are most likely to be disproportionately affected
by attendees with impaired executive functioning. We'll discuss how
this truth could impact the expertise required by your inclusion team.
We'll explore the ways in which the environments where ministry takes
place can help support all attendees, including children and adults
who struggle with self-control. We'll look at how to adapt our styles of
teaching and communication with an audience in mind that has more
difficulty learning and applying important concepts from Scripture,
and how to overcome the challenges involved with helping persons who
struggle with self-discipline to become more consistent in pursuing
spiritual growth.

Who Needs to Be Part of Your Inclusion Team?

The brain pathways involved in mediating the key executive functions (see chapter 4) don't fully mature until young adults enter their
early to mid-twenties. A large majority of those who will demonstrate
problems with self-control in church will be served in your children's
and student ministry departments. For many children with ADHD,
their challenges resulting from hyperactivity and impulsivity dimin-
ish over time. The pastors, staff members, and key volunteers serving
in those departments need to assume leadership for this component

of your inclusion plan. Your team may also seek ideas and support from teachers and other school personnel from your church who have special education experience. You could ask for their advice when considering classroom design for kids who struggle with self-control. Their experience in managing the behavior of kids with executive functioning deficits for six to seven hours in a highly stimulating group situation is likely to be invaluable to your children's ministry staff and volunteers.

Does your church have an adoption ministry or a foster care ministry? If you do, someone involved in the leadership of these ministries should be part of your inclusion team. The children being raised in families served by those ministries have a substantially higher risk of mental health and developmental disabilities associated with compromised executive functioning—ADHD, PTSD, fetal alcohol exposure, mood disorders, and psychotic illness. Some of the most passionate church leaders I've met around the need for more effective mental health inclusion ministry are those who have personal experience with adoption or foster care and have come to recognize that love isn't always enough to change the behavior of a child.

Making Our Ministry Environments More Welcoming

As you consider how to make your church's ministry environments more welcoming to persons who struggle with executive functioning skills, remember that the more information they need to process, the greater their challenges in maintaining self-control and the less likely they will be to remember and internalize important information. Recall the analogy used in chapter 4 in which the brain of someone who struggles with self-control was compared to an older computer short on memory, with too many apps running at once? The first reaction of many church leaders to kids with short attention spans is to pack as much sensory and visual stimulation into their ministry environments as they possibly can—vibrant colors, bright lights, loud music, and custom-designed indoor playgrounds. The environments that kids with well-developed self-control experience as fun and engaging have the same effect on the brain of a kid with ADHD as opening five additional memory-sucking apps while streaming high-definition video on that old computer—there's a good possibility something will crash! What will crash is the child's capacity for managing their behavior. Our goal in designing ministry environments for persons who have executive functioning weaknesses is to create ones that are *engaging*, but not overwhelming.

In the earlier discussion of executive functioning, I noted how important it is to eliminate potential sources of distraction to help our guests concentrate on the most important tasks in that moment. Let's look at a few critical times during church activities when supervision and structure are especially important for children and teens at risk for aggressive behavior.

Transition periods before and after church activities. Staff and volunteers are often distracted by other adults. Commotion resulting from people arriving and leaving and multiple conversations taking place is unsettling to kids who struggle with self-control. There's often no organized activity immediately before and after services to hold the attention of kids who function better when busy, nor is anyone typically keeping an eye on minor provocations between kids that can escalate.

When kids are moving from one physical space to another. Kids with executive functioning deficits may overreact to peers in noisy hallways as they go from one activity to another. A helpful accommodation for kids who are highly reactive during transitions is to send them ahead with another volunteer while the hallways are relatively quiet to help prepare for the next activity.

After high-energy ministry activities. Kids who have executive functioning deficits experience more difficulty settling down in the aftermath of highly stimulating activities than their peers do. If your programming attracts many such kids, your inclusion team could consider scheduling high-energy activities toward the end of their time at church.

Chasing Shiny Objects

In contrast to our other barriers to church participation, persons who struggle from mental health-related executive functioning deficits often experience less difficulty with the *initial experience* of attending church but more difficulty *maintaining* involvement with church. The trajectory of their spiritual growth is often more erratic than that of their peers, and they often experience more difficulty internalizing their faith.

Let's explore some of the challenges they may experience in your church's discipleship programming, and share ideas for keeping them engaged in a spiritual growth process.

Persons with executive functioning deficits are likely to be over-represented among church hoppers. Because they struggle to sustain motivation in familiar activities and routines, they may find themselves drawn to the new preacher in town or seek out the church with the hot new praise band they heard about from a friend. They are more influenced by emotion and environment and more likely to describe intense experiences in novel, spiritually rich environments. They're the kids who get saved at the end of their summer mission trip or the adults who come forward in response to the visiting evangelist's altar call, but who fall off the wagon in terms of living their faith once they're outside the context in which their spiritual experience occurred. They'll skip from church to church or event to event seeking to recapture the spiritual high they remember from a worship service, retreat, or conference. They are often described as exhibiting a "roller-coaster spirituality"— lots of peak experiences followed by lots of lows and little consistency in spiritual growth.

One approach to discipleship with persons with executive functioning deficits is to engage them in the ministries that are more participatory, action oriented, and relational. They're more likely to have positive experiences in activities that involve more doing than talking. Our ministry was consulted by a church struggling with a middle school group in which nine of the sixteen boys had been diagnosed with

ADHD. They were expected to sit in a circle and answer discussion questions posed by group leaders, as their female peers did every Sunday evening. I asked the ministry leaders to consider whether their group might be more successful if the boys discussed the questions with them while loading trucks at the church's food bank.

Another challenge to spiritual growth among persons with executive functioning deficits is a lack of self-discipline. They may resolve to study the Bible from beginning to end but give up when their reading becomes tedious or the content seems less easy to apply. The difficulty they experience in delaying gratification hinders pursuit of long-term spiritual outcomes. Relationships are critically important in overcoming this challenge. Persons with these deficits need friendships with mature Christians who will reach out to them if they're absent from church, their small group, or their Bible study. They need spiritual workout buddies. In the same way that persons who struggle with self-discipline invite friends to come with them to the gym when they're pursuing a physical fitness regimen, they often need the accountability that comes from pursuing spiritual disciplines together with a friend or a circle of friends. Any steps your church takes to systematically follow up with inconsistent attendees and connect them relationally with spiritually mature members helps everyone while providing a disproportionate benefit to persons with mental health conditions that impact their capacity for self-discipline.

Clarify What's Critical

Another issue to consider in incorporating persons with executive functioning deficits into your discipleship strategy is to identify and clearly communicate the activities your church considers most critical for an adult or child on the pathway to spiritual growth.

Would a visitor to your church have a clear understanding of the most important steps they need to take to grow in faith within their first few visits? I suspect the answer to that question in most churches is no. I raise this question because persons who struggle with executive functioning will benefit greatly from a simple discipleship plan. They often struggle to identify priorities. The more alternatives they're presented, the more difficulty they'll have selecting and pursuing a course of action. Identify the two or three most critical ministry activities for spiritual growth at your church and support the participation of visitors and regular attendees who struggle with self-discipline in those activities. This is another strategy that will benefit your entire congregation but will disproportionately benefit members who have executive functioning deficits.

Communicating with Persons with Executive Functioning Deficits

We described earlier some of the challenges persons with executive functioning deficits experience with memory. They often have more difficulty remembering lists or directions and applying concepts learned in one setting to problems they encounter in a different setting. Let's explore how we might modify our approaches to teaching and communication with their weaknesses in mind.

An important—and frequently overlooked—component of a church communication strategy is signage. Consider the challenges someone who struggles to remember multi-step directions might face in finding their way around on their first few visits to a church. Suppose a parent with a condition such as ADHD, which affects their ability to remember directions, has a child with similar problems. The child may be excited about exploring an interesting new space, while the parent is trying to monitor their child's behavior and trying to figure out where they need to go. Is the signage that directs the parent from the parking lot into your building clear? Can they get to where they need to go inside the church without having to stop and ask for directions—directions they probably won't remember? Clear signage with simple directions contributes to a positive first impression among visitors who struggle to navigate unfamiliar places.

Consider your strategy for communicating important teaching

across your church's ministry environments. What do you most want someone to remember after they attend a worship service, Sunday school class, or Bible study? Persons with executive functioning deficits often pay attention to *too many things* to the exclusion of the *most important thing*.

Many teens and young adults with ADHD in my practice frequently get various forms of accommodations at school. They can get a copy of class notes or a study guide that highlights the most important points of the teacher's message. How can your church create a resource that promotes attentiveness to the teacher and facilitates retention of key concepts? A church in my community provides a bulletin insert for each week's sermon in which the message's main points are printed out with blank spaces replacing key words. The task of filling in the blanks during the sermon has been shown to enhance attention to the speaker and retention of key teaching points for listeners.

Andy Stanley and the members of his team at North Point Ministries have developed an approach to communication well suited for children and adults with executive functioning deficits. The principles of North Point's communication approach are outlined in Stanley's book titled *Communicating for a Change*. Andy builds his teaching around the most important *insight* he wants his listeners to take away from his message and the most important *action* he wants them to take in response.[3] Reggie Joiner, the former family ministry director at North Point and founder of the Orange Conference, reminds children's and student ministry leaders that "all Scripture *is* equally inspired by God, but all Scripture is *not* equally important."[4] He encourages them to focus on the "irreducible minimums," or core truths in Scripture.[5]

Let's touch on one more issue related to communication that your team could address in your inclusion plan—the need to create alternative electronic pathways for children's and student ministry teams to share resources directly with families.

Many years ago, we hosted a team of neuropsychology students in our practice who were conducting research on memory and executive functioning. One of their key findings was that persons with executive functioning deficits associated with ADHD often did very well at completing tasks required every day at their job or school, but failed miserably at organizing and remembering tasks that weren't part of a daily routine. The application here for our churches is that kids and adults have much more difficulty remembering to bring their Bibles—or other papers or materials—to and from church than they do in remembering items they organize every day. Ministry leaders can't rely on kids with executive functioning weaknesses to get necessary papers or family ministry resources back to parents, and they can't expect parents with similar weaknesses who are separated or divorced to share resources with one another. If your church employs a family ministry approach to discipleship with your children and teens in which parents are encouraged to discuss themes raised during weekend worship services and Sunday school throughout the week, you need to acquire technology that will allow you to notify parents directly when you have resources to share—and you need to be able to make those resources available to parents electronically.

If schools have recognized the need to make required forms, textbooks, and homework assignments available online for forgetful students—even when school is part of their daily routine *and* kids are surrounded by trained professionals—how much greater is the need for such resources at church?

Education and Support for Families of Children Who Struggle with Self-Control

In upcoming chapters on sensory processing and social isolation, I'll discuss several strategies for supporting families of children who struggle with self-control. I'd like to share two ideas here for providing education and support that are specific for families of children and adults who have executive functioning deficits.

I have a very difficult time finding support groups for families in my practice in which a child or parent has ADHD. Support groups are typically started by family members or spouses of someone with ADHD. Groups tend to be short-lived because the founders don't have the capacity to sustain the groups without some organizational support, given the other demands they face as caregivers. Founders may have connections with a circle of friends with similar needs. Once the needs of the original group members are met, there may not be enough willpower to sustain the group or a ready supply of families to replenish the group.

Churches can provide organizational and clerical support, along with a permanent home for ADHD support groups. Since one in nine school-age children will be treated for ADHD, churches with busy children's and student ministries represent a steady source of families for an education and support group.

We briefly touched on the importance of inviting adoption ministry and foster care ministry leaders into your mental health inclusion process. Christian families who have been called to these ministries are especially in need of encouragement of support. Where do they turn for help when the children in their care demonstrate the behavior problems typical of kids who have been exposed to trauma, abuse, and neglect, and when they belong to a church that interprets such behavior as a reflection of poor parenting?

Churches interested in supporting families who serve in adoption or foster care ministries might consider providing "Empowered To Connect Parent Training," a biblically based training model developed at Texas Christian University for parents of adoptive and foster children.[6] Empowered To Connect offers a six-session training model for families considering adoption or foster care, and a nine-session model for parents who have already adopted. Sessions last for two hours, follow a set curriculum, and are led by parents, adoption, or foster care ministry leaders who have completed a "Train the Trainer" module or professionals who were trained through the TCU Institute of Child Development.

RESPONSIBILITY FOR MINISTRY

Individuals with executive functioning deficits such as ADHD often possess gifts and talents that are of great benefit in ministry. They may have a greater willingness to take chances for God than do people who have more self-control. They may have great energy and enthusiasm for ministry ideas that capture their hearts and imagination. They may be very effective on ministry teams where others have complementary gifts of administration and organization. Their lack of inhibitions often helps them to be very effective in sharing the gospel. While my observations of church leaders may reflect a referral bias among churches that seek the services of Key Ministry, I suspect a disproportionate number of pastors—especially senior pastors and youth pastors—have features of ADHD.

Many years ago, I sat in my office on a Saturday morning with the parents of two young boys with severe ADHD. They became emotional as they described their experiences attending worship services with their boys prior to discovering the church my family and I attend. They were later invited to share their stories at our church during a Disability Sunday worship service. The mother shared this observation that I've often used in Key Ministry training: *People in the church believe they can tell when a disability ends and bad parenting begins.*

There's a happy ending to the story. Both boys grew up in our church, participated in our ministries for children and teens, went off to college, graduated, and are very successful. The older of the two boys moved back to town, got married, is active in his church, and serves Christian organizations through his current job.

The children and families we are most likely to judge at church are often the people God uses to advance his mission in the world. Let's seek to welcome them and offer them the opportunity to use their gifts and talents for the benefit of the church as we seek to be the hands and feet of Jesus in the world.

NINE

Overcoming Sensory Processing Differences

I am very nervous about joining a new church because of the experiences I have had in church before. I so find the loud rock concert type services completely overwhelming. However, the social aspects at the quieter services are just as overwhelming as some very perky person pounces in on me. Although I typically like structure and routine, I do enjoy contemporary (less high services) for connecting with God. In addition, there is all that small talk around swarms of people wearing all sorts of perfume who do not understand when I talk loudly, change topics, or suddenly get distracted.

SYDNEY (NOT HER REAL NAME)

These words were written by a follower of Key Ministry's blog for churches in response to a post on sensory processing issues at church. Her experiences at church are typical of the descriptions I hear from my patients and their families after attending large group events.

This chapter on sensory processing is positioned between our discussions of executive functioning and social communication, because children and adults with sensory processing differences often experience concomitant difficulties with executive functioning and social communication, and the intervention strategies recommended for persons with sensory processing differences will likely be applicable for persons with the other two conditions.

Readers familiar with features of common mental health conditions will recognize that sensory processing issues are very common among persons with autism spectrum disorders, but are increasingly recognized in association with ADHD and anxiety disorders and are sometimes present in the absence of any diagnosed mental health condition. That's a good reminder that any effective mental health inclusion strategy shouldn't require knowing the diagnoses of those served by your ministry.

DEVELOPING A SENSORY-FRIENDLY INCLUSION STRATEGY

The most significant strategy for including persons with sensory processing differences involves a thorough review of your key facilities and ministry environments to identify sources of excessive sensory stimulation that can be remedied at a modest cost and minimal disruption to worship experiences and church traditions. We'll look at people who could advise your inclusion team about how to make your facilities more sensory friendly, share an outside-the-box communication strategy for ministering to families of kids with sensory processing issues, and present your church with an opportunity for meeting a practical need in your community while signaling your willingness to welcome children and adults who have sensory processing differences.

Sensory-Friendly Ministry Environments

Our ministry was fortunate to have a staff member for several years (Harmony Hensley) who worked as an interior designer prior to entering ministry. She wrote several posts for Key Ministry's Church4EveryChild blog on creating welcoming ministry environments for kids with disabilities.[1] Some of the ideas presented here are drawn from Harmony's blog posts; others are my own. Collectively, they can serve as a checklist for your church's ministry teams in evaluating spaces where they offer ministry.

Lighting. Fluorescent lighting is cost-effective and floods a space with light. In one small study, fluorescent light was shown to worsen repetitive behaviors when compared to incandescent light of similar intensity among a sample of children with autism spectrum disorders.[2] The harshness of fluorescent lighting may be greater in spaces where light is easily reflected by other surfaces, including shiny linoleum floors. Inexpensive fluorescent light filters are available that diffuse the harsh glare while reducing flickering and eye strain. Another approach to reducing the harshness of your lighting involves removing some fluorescent bulbs. Traditional lamp lighting (think floor lamps and table lamps) can create a more soothing environment while still offering plenty of task lighting. Recessed lighting may be an alternative to fluorescent lights in new construction or renovation of existing facilities.

Flooring. Churches often use linoleum or other hard surface flooring in children's ministry and student ministry areas because these materials are easier to maintain. The downside for children and teens with sensory processing differences is that sound reverberates off hard flooring. Acoustics in carpeted rooms are generally more sensory friendly. Carpet tiles often improve the acoustics of a room and are easily replaced if stained or soiled. Area rugs may absorb some of the excess sound in rooms with hard floors and offer more comfortable seating for children during group lessons.

Window treatments. Window treatments impact the amount of light in your ministry spaces while serving as buffers to the level of sound. Blinds allow you to control the amount of light in your spaces while minimizing potential distractions for children and adults who struggle to maintain focus and attention.

Wall color. Churches often go overboard in their use of color in spaces designed for children. Walls are often painted in the most vibrant primary colors imaginable, and murals are common in hallways. Consider replacing primary colors (fire engine red, Big Bird yellow, Kelly green) with richer jewel tone colors.

Fragrance-free zones. The church that my family and I attend has a thriving special needs ministry with an overrepresentation of children and adults who have sensory processing differences. The special needs ministry team repurposed the comfortable (and soundproofed) space that previously served as the cry room as a fragrance-free zone for adults and children.

Sound. The movie industry standard for sound calibration is set at 85 decibels.[3] The US Occupational Safety and Health Administration mandates ear protection for workers spending eight or more hours per day in environments where the noise level exceeds 90 decibels.[4]

Consider that many theatre chains have recognized the need to offer sensory-friendly screenings of popular films because audience members with autism spectrum disorders and sensory processing differences don't tolerate the typical sound volume during movies. Your inclusion team should make use of free cell phone apps to measure the level of noise at different room locations during your children's, student, and adult worship services and adjust the volume accordingly. If you find areas in your worship spaces that are more acoustically friendly to persons with sensory processing differences, help attendees who could benefit to find those areas.

Seating. Unless your church has an extraordinary endowment, your team is unlikely to be able to do much to change the seating in your primary worship space. Older, more traditional churches typically feature hard-backed wooden pews. More modern churches may rely on portable seating so that large gathering spaces can be used for a variety of activities. In examining your ministry environments, your team will want to consider whether comfortable seating is available for children and adults with sensory processing differences. In children's ministry spaces, "comfortable" seating might consist of beanbag chairs or balance ball chairs on the periphery of the room. Couches are a seating option in many student ministry spaces. Many of the more contemporary churches I've visited in recent years have set aside spaces for attendees to gather outside of the main worship center, featuring comfortable seating with the service displayed on video monitors with adjustable volume controls.

In the community where my family and I live, the churches that have built or remodeled their worship centers in the last ten years have switched from pews to theatre-style seating. The theatre seating ensures that persons with sensory processing differences will be able to maintain space between themselves and the person seated next to them.

Who Can Help Us?

In our discussion on the composition of the inclusion team in chapter 5, we suggested adding an interior designer and occupational therapist to the team specifically for their contributions in modifying ministry environments. What should you do if your team doesn't have access to someone with that background or skill set?

Do you have any parents of children with sensory processing issues in your church? They're likely to be adept at recognizing sources of excessive sensory stimulation. If you don't have anyone in your church with known sensory processing issues, consider reaching out to directors of special needs ministries in nearby churches. They'll have a keen appreciation of potential triggers for guests and regular attendees at risk for sensory overload.

Where Should We Start?

The idea of systematically reviewing all your ministry facilities may seem overwhelming. If the idea itself doesn't seem overwhelming, the cost of addressing *all* sources of excessive sensory stimulation will be! If I were to focus on three areas in your church to make more sensory friendly, I'd start with entrances, spaces where worship services take place (children and adults), and spaces where children's and student ministry activities occur. Establishing a sensory-friendly entrance to your church is a relatively easy first step in an inclusion plan.

THE ULTIMATE SENSORY-FRIENDLY WORSHIP SERVICE

Several years ago, our ministry experimented with an online church platform as an alternative for families of kids with disabilities. We found some of our most consistent online attendees were families in which one or more members experienced sensory processing differences. One parent noted their ability to adjust the volume of the worship music on the TV in their living room enabled them to worship together as a family. Online worship services, Christian education programs, and small groups afford individuals with sensory processing differences the opportunity to experience church in the environments that work best for them.

OFFERING PRACTICAL HELP TO YOUR COMMUNITY

I'd like to share two wonderful ideas generated by disability ministry leaders with some connection to our Key Ministry team for church-sponsored events and activities targeting the needs of families of children with sensory processing differences.

One of our former board members is a special education teacher by training who recognized that kids with sensory issues were missing out on her church's Vacation Bible School, an enormously popular event each summer that drew hundreds of kids to her church. She approached church leaders about developing a one-day, sensory-friendly VBS experience for kids in her community who wouldn't participate in the week-long program because they couldn't tolerate the stimulation. Her church asked their 160 teen VBS volunteers who served in the week-long program to come back for a sixth day on Saturday for the kids with sensory needs and promoted the event to other churches and schools across their region. Much to the surprise of our former colleague, the kids who volunteered to serve and their families were more effective at marketing the event than her church's communication team. The volunteers and their families enthusiastically extended personal invitations to their friends and neighbors who would benefit. The parents of kids who participated were amazed by the church's tangible demonstration of the value they placed on their children participating in VBS. The special needs ministry of another church in our area now offers their entire VBS program in a sensory-friendly format in the evenings during the week their traditional program is offered during the morning.

Another creative idea for serving the needs of children and adults with sensory processing differences resulted from one family's disastrous attempt to go to the movies during a Christmas break.

Emily Colson is an award-winning author and disability ministry advocate who contributes to *Not Alone*, Key Ministry's blog for families of kids with disabilities. Emily has written extensively about her experiences in raising a son (Max) with autism, and the ways in which Max's disability reveals something about the people he touches. Several years ago, Emily and her stepmom accompanied Max to a screening of *The Muppet Movie*. He began shrieking in response to the eardrum-shattering volume of the previews; he yelled out, "I want to go home!" after being startled by the increased sound volume as the feature began. The audience at the movie began to heckle Max and responded with thunderous applause as Max and his family left the theatre.

Emily's blog post went viral and generated lots of media attention as families identified with her family's experience at the theater.[5] But that wasn't the end of the story.

Another family from Emily's church came up with the idea of renting out an entire theatre so Max would be able to enjoy a sensory-friendly showing of the movie. Their pastor embraced the idea of hosting a special screening of the movie for Max and other families like his, with the people of the church filling the remaining seats to show their support. Emily described the scene at the end of the movie in another post:

> As the movie came to a close, the Muppets began to sing what was clearly the grand finale. No one wanted the evening to end. Suddenly, people flooded into the aisles as if they were leaving. But instead, they began to dance. Everyone free. No armor. No barriers between us.
>
> I looked around in awe and wondered if this is what Jesus envisioned when he said, *"Love one another."* When He spoke those words, did he picture this very moment in a theater, when love would take our breath away and lift us out of our seats? When His love would win? God's story of redemption is written across our lives over and over again.[6]

The people of Emily's church identified a way to affirm her family's value while blessing other families in their community through sponsoring a sensory-friendly movie experience. There's no reason your church can't do the same for families in your community.

You've likely noticed more references in this chapter on sensory processing to strategies associated with special needs ministry than in any other chapter in the book. While it's true that many persons with intellectual or developmental disabilities referred to as "special needs" experience sensory processing issues, and that we in the church can learn much from the experience of our colleagues in special needs ministry, a much larger population will benefit from your inclusion team's attempts to create more sensory-friendly ministry environments than would be served through an identified special needs ministry.

TEN

Overcoming Social Communication Challenges

They devoted themselves to the apostles' teaching and to fellowship, to the breaking of bread and to prayer . . . All the believers were together and had everything in common. They sold property and possessions to give to anyone who had need. Every day they continued to meet together in the temple courts. They broke bread in their homes and ate together with glad and sincere hearts, praising God and enjoying the favor of all the people.

ACTS 2:42, 44–47

Churches are hubs of social activity. In Acts 2, the biblical writer Luke describes the typical activities of the early church—and it involves a lot of social interaction! They ate together, shared everything, and gathered together daily. Church isn't something we do by ourselves. Jesus emphasized the importance of Christian community when he said, "Where two or three gather in my name, there am I with them"

(Matthew 18:20). All Christian churches regularly gather for worship services. Many people crave the social interactions and relationships available through involvement in the church.

Survey data supports the idea that desire for community is one of the top reasons people report for attending church.[1] Studies have identified friendliness of members and fellowship as key reasons for choosing a church and maintaining a high level of involvement at church.[2] We need other people who share our beliefs to provide encouragement, accountability, and support. Involvement in community through small groups and proclaiming the gospel through service to others are broadly accepted as essential catalysts for spiritual growth. Most Protestant churches and a growing number of Roman Catholic churches emphasize participation in small group community experiences.

Ed Stetzer, a prominent author, blogger, pastor, and church strategist, summarizes the importance of community in the local church:

> Community matters. It's a biblical non-negotiable. Transformation is not an individual task. No Christian is an island. The model Jesus gave us for disciple making is one of shared experience and learning in community. Christ did life together with his disciples, and he expects us to undergo life transformation as a community.[3]

Your church's model for assimilating newcomers may work well for many of your visitors, but imagine the challenges a child or adult would experience when they try to connect with people at your church with diminished ability to process social cues. They may misinterpret the body language or facial expressions of people around them. They may fail to detect sarcasm in conversations or detect subtle changes in the meaning of speech reflected through vocal tone or inflection. They may not have a good sense of the appropriate thing to say or do in unfamiliar social situations. The bottom line is they're likely to flounder with the interactions common to church activities.

Carlyle King is a Christian with a physical disability and Asperger syndrome who advocates for persons in the church with disabilities affecting social communication. He shared this description of what church is like for someone like himself:

> I end up going to church feeling like I'm walking blindfolded in a minefield, because if I run into a problem, everyone will abandon me and that makes ministering to those adults like me that much harder. I hear this hurt from others constantly, and they tell me that a God with people like that isn't worth following. I understand that. I've been there myself. Why are we the outcasts?

Carlyle's poignant observations reflect two important observations essential for church leaders seeking to minister with persons with disorders affecting social communication. First, *most kids and adults who struggle to connect in social environments desire authentic friendships in which they can be known, understood, and valued.* They want to be part of a larger community where they use their gifts and talents alongside others in support of a larger cause, and they want to share their lives with others. Second, *despite the struggles many children and adults experience in church life, they still desperately want to belong to a church.* Some overcome their discomfort with social interaction and make vital contributions to the work of their local churches.

How can our churches do a better job of welcoming people like Carlyle?

STRATEGIES FOR WELCOMING PERSONS WITH SOCIAL COMMUNICATION DEFICITS

In this chapter, I'll examine four important considerations in an inclusion strategy for supporting children and adults who struggle in social situations:

- accommodations to discipleship strategies designed around groups
- the importance of educating kids and families about the impact of bullying
- alternative communication strategies
- how to meet one of their most heartfelt needs—friendship

Friendship before Discipleship?

One of the greatest obstacles to spiritual growth in persons with conditions impacting social communication is getting them to come to church in the first place, given their experiences with church and individual Christians.

Children and adults who struggle with social communication are frequent objects of bullying at school or work, and they're more "acceptable" targets for harassment within their peer culture than persons with more obvious disabilities.

They are also quick to recognize hypocrisy. All too often, I encounter children and adults who conclude that Christianity is inauthentic when peers who call themselves "Christian" are insensitive or cruel in their day-to-day interactions.

Many persons with social communication challenges also experience *cognitive rigidity*—an inability to consider alternatives to a situation, alternative viewpoints for interpreting the meaning of actions or events, or innovative solutions for problems. A simpler way of describing cognitive rigidity is to think of someone with a propensity to get stuck. They get a picture in their mind of how they expect situations to unfold, and once they form a judgment or opinion, their opinion is often set in concrete. They are often prone to all-or-nothing thinking. They tend to use words such as *always* or *never* in describing other people, institutions, and potential courses of action. One negative experience of church or of Christians—and their experience becomes representative of *all* churches or Christians. The takeaway for ministry leaders is we need all who represent the church to be aware of the long-lasting impact their cruel or insensitive words may have on others.

Friendship as Outreach Ministry

Mike Woods, who served as one of Key Ministry's church consultants and director of the Special Friends Ministry at First Baptist Church in Orlando, writes, "In the Gospels, Jesus presents us with a radically different perception of friendship. Jesus befriended those who were cast out by society—the tax collectors, the blind, lepers, the poor, the mentally ill, harlots, all those who were in many respects radically unlike himself."[4]

Churches can offer great comfort to persons who struggle with social isolation through extending opportunities for friendship.

In chapter 1, I referenced Ben Conner's work with teens and young adults with autism spectrum disorders. He emphasized the propensity of our culture to overlook their unique gifts and talents and to minimize their value as friends. The parents of kids I see in my practice desperately want their children to be sought out as companions by their peers. We need to constantly remind the families in our churches to encourage their kids to sit with peers who are alone in the cafeteria or on the school bus and to choose for their team the kid who never gets picked on the playground. Adults need to check in from time to time with more introverted friends and be intentional in pursuing relationships with persons who cross their paths.

We also need to be intentional in teaching our kids to be considerate of peers who may be less socially adept. Children's and student ministry leaders may assume that their kids spend lots of time in school learning about the impact of bullying. Given the devastating effects of bullying done by Christians on Christ's reputation and the reputation of his church, I would encourage all churches, *especially* churches with an intentional disability inclusion ministry, to address bullying in the context of church. Key Ministry's Vimeo page features an excellent presentation for ministry leaders by two of our former staff members, Katie Wetherbee and Rebecca Hamilton, outlining strategies for preventing bullying at church.[5]

Alternative Approaches to Spiritual Growth

Inclusion is not an all-or-nothing proposition. Partial inclusion of children and teens who struggle with social skills may be an option. Depending on the nature of your church's ministry environments, the adult worship service may be a better experience for kids with significant social skill deficits. Kids may not experience the same pressures for social interaction in the worship service with grown-ups. Teens could come to an adult worship service but feel uncomfortable doing a house group. That's OK. What's important is that your church establishes a connection with the family and is positioned to come alongside the parents as they direct the spiritual growth of their children.

Parents of children with social communication difficulties often report that their children relate more easily to adults than to peers. Adults tend to be more tolerant of a broader range of social behaviors and quicker to identify areas of common interest. Your inclusion team can offer families of children and teens who struggle to fit in with their same-age peers at church the option of having their child do an educational activity with a familiar adult with or without a friend or two. Providing opportunities for kids with social skill deficits to serve alongside adults helps them grow in confidence as they tap into their gifts and abilities, promotes the development of spiritual friendships, and helps them internalize the understanding that they have a valuable role to play in the church.

Adults who struggle with the social demands of church may respond better to one-on-one discipleship opportunities. Consider offering options for Bible studies or small group studies either directly to individuals or in groups composed of two or three peers of the same sex. The ancient practice of pairing individuals with a *spiritual direc-tor*—a mature Christian who helps a fellow believer to discern what the Holy Spirit is doing and saying and to act on that discernment, drawing nearer to God in Christ—is an alternative approach in churches where discipleship largely occurs in groups.[6]

Church Communication Strategies

Do you ever find yourself avoiding online discussions because you're afraid your comments on a blog or social media platform will be misunderstood because someone reading your words can't process the full meaning of what you're saying without being able to see and hear you? You're now on a level playing field with someone who has a social communication disorder.

I've observed that many teens in my practice with disorders impacting social communication depend on texting and instant messaging as a social lifeline. Online gaming may be one of their most meaningful social outlets. They gravitate to technology that puts them on a level playing field with more neurotypical peers because it minimizes the need to process nonverbal social cues and affords them greater ability to contemplate responses to comments and statements from peers.

In the earlier discussion of inclusion strategies for persons with anxiety, I suggested that mental health inclusion teams create electronic alternatives for communicating with pastors, church staff, and volunteers—providing an electronic option for every interaction currently done by phone. Electronic communication options will also support the needs of persons with compromised social communication ability, but for a different reason. Persons with anxiety avoid telephones because of personal discomfort, whereas folks with social communication disorders avoid them because they're at a relative disadvantage versus other forms of electronic communication that don't require an immediate face-to-face response. Perhaps they can attend your church through an online worship experience accompanied by an interactive chat guided by a pastor or ministry leader if your services are streamed live over the web.

As we conclude, here's a summary of the key components of a strategy for including children and adults who have social skill deficits at church:

- Remember that most children and adults can master the necessary social skills for navigating our ministry environments. Our responsibility as leaders is to demonstrate empathy and consideration through anticipating the challenges they may encounter when joining our ministry activities and experiences.

- Keep in mind that your ministry strategies must afford the flexibility that supports alternative approaches to discipleship when programs and activities that work for most attendees aren't a good fit with a person's unique gifts, talents, and weaknesses.
- We need to reflect the value for relationship that Jesus demonstrated throughout his earthly ministry and ultimately in his death on the cross and subsequent resurrection.
- Finally, we need to be mindful (and make our children mindful) of the impact our words and actions have on Jesus' reputation among those who form lasting impressions of Jesus based on their experiences of us.

ELEVEN

Overcoming Social Isolation

Who shall separate us from the love of Christ? Shall trouble or hardship or persecution or famine or nakedness or danger or sword?

ROMANS 8:35

Mental illness contributes to social isolation, and social isolation is a risk factor for mental illness. It's all too easy for individuals with mental illness and their families to find themselves trapped in a downward spiral—persons with depression retreat from the world as they lose interest in activities they used to enjoy; the anxious avoid the scrutiny of others; kids with ADHD drive friends away through their anger and impulsiveness; men and women with schizophrenia withdraw into their misperceptions and delusions; and adults with personality disorders leave a trail of fractured relationships in their wake—every broken relationship further increasing the risk for more episodes of more serious illness in the future.

I'm reminded of the picture that King David casts of the "pit" in Psalm 40:1–2:

> I waited patiently for the Lord;
>> he turned to me and heard my cry.
> He lifted me out of the slimy pit,
>> out of the mud and mire;
> he set my feet on a rock
>> and gave me a firm place to stand.

The bottom line is that a large segment of the child and adult population in the United States experiences mental health conditions that contribute enormously to social isolation. We as the church need to do our part in helping pull them out of the pit. One reason the church needs to act is that it's simply the right thing to do. Another reason is that Jesus' last words to his children before returning to heaven say something about us *going to* people who aren't yet part of his family with the good news of the gospel. We in the church are the ones given the responsibility for reaching out and building the relationships necessary for introducing others to Jesus.

We need to become far more intentional in our outreach efforts to individuals and families impacted by mental illness because it's hard for families to be invited to church when they don't know anyone who regularly attends church. They aren't coming to us; we need to go to them. When we do, we mirror the grace God extends to us. We have a relationship with God because God's Son did something for us that we couldn't possibly do for ourselves.

AN INCLUSION STRATEGY FOR OVERCOMING SOCIAL ISOLATION

The way we overcome isolation is through promoting *connectedness*. We need to consider how to use each of our inclusion strategies to promote connectedness. Who can you find for your church's mental health inclusion team who can identify and mobilize persons with established connections within the mental health community to leverage those connections on behalf of the church? How does your inclusion team stay connected with and mobilize your foot soldiers in the church's guerrilla warfare to win over hearts and souls for Jesus—your members and regular attendees who have relationships with kids and adults in homes impacted by mental illness where no one yet knows Jesus? How do we use the tools of modern technology to make introductions that lead to relationships? Can we establish new, online expressions of Christian community? What would "mission trips" to families touched by mental illness look like? Are there ways of bringing together people with mental illness who are already part of the church with those outside of the church to learn and grow together?

Leveraging Your Church's Social Networks

Your mental health inclusion team doesn't need to include every person in your church whom God has already positioned to regularly interact with children, adults, and families impacted by mental illness, but your team does need someone capable of identifying them, putting in place the required systems to organize and develop lines of communication with them, and casting your team's vision for a mental health initiative. These responsibilities are likely to rest with your church's ministerial and support staff.

To help you find persons in your church who regularly contact individuals or families affected by mental illness, ask yourself these questions:

Do we have attendees . . .

- who are employed by our community's mental health system?
- who work in private counseling offices or psychiatry practices, even in clerical or support positions?
- who work in group homes housing adults or children with mental illness?
- who work in primary care (Family Medicine, Internal Medicine, Pediatrics, Obstetrics/Gynecology) medical practices?

- who serve in the special education departments of local schools?
- who are involved with our area's child or adult protective services?
- who are involved with our community's adoption agencies or foster care providers?

Each member or regular attender who serves in one of these capacities represents a potential ambassador of your church to the mental health community. They're likely to be your most effective—and cost-efficient—marketing team.

Go and Tell versus Come and See

The qualities of your ministry environments are irrelevant in the absence of meaningful relationships between your people and individuals impacted by mental illness outside the church. Your inclusion team could consider ways of taking ministry into the environments where persons with mental illness are already comfortable. How could you provide practical support to adults with severe mental illness and their families so they can keep living at home? Could small groups within your church "adopt" families within your community of children with significant mental illnesses? In this "relational respite" model, couples or families in a small group take turns providing child care and other supports inside the family's home.

In the chapter describing the seven inclusion strategies, you were introduced to Christian models for mental health education and support groups. What if your church took your education and support groups to places in your community where persons with mental illness already gather? Is there a private mental health clinic you could partner with in hosting Grace Groups or Fresh Hope Groups organized and promoted by your church's inclusion team?

An outwardly focused mental health inclusion initiative can embrace urgent but unmet needs in the local community when the church has the resources to make a difference. While I was writing this chapter, I found myself communicating with a special needs ministry director about the challenges of families of preschoolers in need of psychiatric hospitalization because of extremely dangerous or self-injurious behaviors. In many regions of the country, preschoolers and their parents all too often find themselves "boarding" in local emergency rooms for days while waiting for a hospital bed. The hospital can't send the child home without twenty-four-hour supervision, which families can't provide for various reasons, including the need for sleep or to go to work. Churches can provide an invaluable service by offering responsible adults (after the necessary background checks and accompanied by appropriate supervision and support) to help families maintain the safety of their young children while they wait for appropriate treatment services.

Your church's capacity for outwardly focused mental health ministry is limited only by your ability to identify unmet needs within your community and the willingness of your people to give of their time and talents to respond to the needs.

Taking Church to Them

If your mental health inclusion team were given an inexpensive opportunity to establish a ministry environment that entered the homes of families in your community without a church, would you pursue it? What if your team could use that environment to introduce those families to key ministry leaders and volunteers within your church? Churches with online campuses that feature live streaming of worship services and "simulated live" services throughout the week can do just that!

An online worship service is an ideal way for churches to introduce themselves to individuals and families in their local communities who are affected by mental illness. Online services are often accompanied by an interactive chat capability that enables pastoral staff and volunteers to pray with participants and connect them with other ministries and resources. Persons who may be anxious or uncomfortable about visiting your church can literally try it out from home! The real benefit of online services when it comes to disability inclusion is the ability to make virtual introductions between folks without a church and people within the church who can provide them with the individualized support they need to worship together with other Christians. With online church, any group home or assisted living center where persons with chronic mental illness live can potentially be converted into a satellite campus.

One way to make persons impacted by mental illness aware of the availability of online church options is through paid or free advertising opportunities on the internet or via social media. Google Grants offers up to $10,000 per month to qualified nonprofits in free advertising via Google AdWords. Facebook allows churches to advertise content to targeted groups in their communities at a modest cost. As an aside, our team at Key Ministry can target readers in identified geographic areas (cities, regions)—using mental health or other disability-related terms—at a cost of five cents per response or less. People who may not intentionally be looking for a church may discover your church when advertisements begin to turn up in the Facebook news feed.

By putting worship services, small group opportunities, and other church activities online and promoting them through social media, you've made it ridiculously easy for your members and regular attendees to share links to your services and special programming directly with their friends and neighbors who could benefit. Folks who may be reluctant to invite a neighbor or coworker to church through a face-to-face invitation can easily forward links to your online worship services and other electronic resources provided by your church. When your leadership team is comfortable with the church's ability to minister effectively with children and adults with mental illness, your communications team could schedule links to your online resources and reminders for members to share with friends, colleagues, and family members who might benefit from your mental health ministry strategy, as well as suggest ways your people can help friends and loved ones impacted by mental illness to experience the love of Christ through their personal ministry.

By no means is the content of an online church campus limited to streamed worship services. There's no reason your church can't host fully interactive online mental health education and support groups. Our ministry quite successfully hosted an online multifamily support group for families of kids with disabilities under the supervision of pastor and author Dr. Lorna Bradley. We've hosted an online book study for more than four hundred participants and have organized multiple online groups through Facebook.

The gospel compels us to reach people through personal relationships. Online relationships are *real relationships*. We have a senior leader who will have worked for Key Ministry for more than a year and a half at the time this book goes to press, and I've never met her in person. Whatever means you use—a communications strategy, an event, or just a knock on the door—the goal is to promote personal connections between those who know Jesus and persons with mental illness so they might be introduced to Jesus as well.

When Should We Host Special Events at Our Church?

I don't mean to imply that we as a church can't put on events in our established facilities that families affected by mental illness will want to attend. A great example is church-based respite events.

As I mentioned in an earlier chapter, parents of children with mental health conditions often experience great difficulty in accessing appropriate child care. When our ministry was training churches to provide respite events as an outreach strategy to families of kids with special needs, more families accessing respite events had children with a primary mental health condition as opposed to intellectual or developmental disabilities. One strategy contributing to the success of the respite events in the mental health community was the decision to include "typical" siblings of kids with disabilities in the events and to provide everyone with their own one-on-one buddy, regardless of their disability status. As a result, kids with primary mental health conditions experienced less stigma around attending, since the event was organized in a way that allowed them to blend in with the typical siblings.

There are compelling reasons for churches to launch a respite ministry. We found that between 25 and 40 percent of families who lacked a church and registered for a respite event would attend a weekend worship service at one of the sites where they obtained respite within twelve months of their initial visit. Another key to successful respite events is using the events to promote relationships between the families providing and receiving respite. This vignette, shared by Libby Peterson, a prominent family ministry leader and former Key Ministry board member, illustrates the concept:

> "So, you mean that we can invite the child we just met at the respite event to our house for my son's birthday party?"
>
> The question was asked at a gathering we held following a respite event at our church. We invited volunteers who served at the event to my house to debrief the respite and talk about connections they had made with the kids.
>
> My answer to that question was an unreserved and totally enthusiastic: "YESSSSSSSSSSSSSSS!"
>
> We held this gathering to begin to cast a vision for a next step in ministry that took ministry outside the walls of the church. I believe ministry happens best when real relationships develop—and we wanted to encourage our families to begin building relationships/friendships with the families they served. Our hope is that through these relationships not only will these families be drawn closer to Christ, but that through these relationships we'd be able to develop relationships with families they know who we don't know or ever see at one of our events. And some real friendships have emerged—and we've learned AGAIN just how much we need each other.[1]

Respite represents a great way for local churches to offer support to families of kids with serious mental conditions, which, when done correctly, helps promote relationships while decreasing social isolation.

If it were easy for individuals and families with mental illness to come to us, they would have already and there would be no need for inclusion teams and initiatives. We're going to have to put in the extra effort to take the first step of reaching out. But in doing so, we'll bring great honor to God our Father and reap the added benefit of making quite a few new friends along the way!

TWELVE

Overcoming Past Church Experience

Know therefore that the LORD your God is God; he is the faithful God, keeping his covenant of love to a thousand generations of those who love him and keep his commandments.

DEUTERONOMY 7:9

While churches and Christian ministries devote vast resources to evangelizing adults, research suggests most adult Christians became Christians in their childhood. The observation that most people who come to Christ do so between the ages of four and fourteen years of age has come to be known as the "4/14 window."[1]

The Barna Group set out to examine factors that contribute to a person coming to faith in Christ. One of their most surprising findings in support of a 4-14 window was that most Christians have come to faith by the age of thirteen, and the odds of someone coming to faith as an adult are less than one in ten.[2]

Having reviewed the research on spiritual development, when our ministry team set out to develop the inclusion model described in this book I envisioned an approach for churches seeking to welcome and include *children and teens* with mental health conditions. I was very familiar with the challenges they experience at church from my day job of the past thirty years. The data clearly suggests that churches are most likely to get the best return on investment from a discipleship standpoint by devoting more resources to children's ministry.

Our organization is well connected in the children's ministry world, and most of the requests we receive for training and assistance come from church staff or volunteers involved with children's, student, family, or special needs ministry departments. The churches that contact us for help in serving specific kids are working with families led by parents who, by and large, have already come to faith in Christ. But upon further reflection, I concluded that any ministry inclusion model that failed to address the needs of each generation in the family was greatly limited in its potential impact.

Mental illness and the Christian faith are both transmitted from generation to generation. The multigenerational nature of the problems presented by mental illness call for a churchwide approach to inclusion. Or to say it another way, we need to think of mental health inclusion ministry as *family ministry*.

Let's take a closer look at the families we're called to serve. We know that children of parents with mental illness are significantly more likely to experience mental illness themselves. An analysis of thirty-three studies examining risk of mental illness among children of parents with severe mental illness (schizophrenia, bipolar disorder, and major depression) reports the following:

- Children of parents with severe mental illness had a 32 percent probability of developing severe mental illness by adulthood. Their risk was roughly 2.5 times greater than controls.
- Children were 3.5 times more likely than controls to develop the same disorder as their parent and nearly twice as likely to develop a different severe illness than controls.
- Children of parents with bipolar disorder are six times more likely to develop schizophrenia than controls.[3]

Another study examining the heritability of disruptive behavior disorders demonstrated that 75 percent of the risk for ADHD is attributable to genetic factors, and the prevalence of ADHD is approximately 30 percent among children of parents with ADHD.[4]

I share this data to illustrate both a problem and an opportunity for the church. While children of parents with mental illness are more likely to themselves experience mental illness, the *most* likely outcome is that they will themselves be free of mental illness. Here are three thoughts for pastors and church leaders as they consider this data:

1. If you can welcome parents with mental illness, you get the privilege of ministering with lots of kids with and without mental illness who fall within the prime 4-14 window.
2. You're likely to have lots of family members without mental illness who can lend support to parents with mental illness in fulfilling their role as primary faith trainers.
3. There are lots of natural points for disrupting multigenerational patterns of church avoidance associated with mental illness.

If we're going to break the cycle, we need an inclusion strategy to get to the parents to support them. We need to be able to welcome parents with mental illness and help them grow spiritually if they're to serve as the primary faith trainers of their children. We must be prepared to welcome and support kids with mental illness if we're to earn the privilege of coming alongside and supporting parents as they seek to raise their kids in the faith. If we can't get to the parents, we need a strategy for resourcing grandparents, extended family members, and, if need be, adoptive and foster parents. We need a long-term approach to overcome our final inclusion barrier—helping more family members affected by mental illness have positive experiences of church to pass down to succeeding generations.

What might such a ministry strategy look like?

A FAMILY-BASED DISCIPLESHIP STRATEGY

Before we dive into the specifics, let's look at additional research that can help guide our approach.

The Search Institute conducted a three-and-a-half-year-long study examining indicators of faith maturity in 2,365 youth, primarily from mainline denominations (Presbyterian Church [USA], United Methodist Church, United Church of Christ, Evangelical Lutheran Church of America, and the Disciples of Christ, with Southern Baptists used as a comparison group). According to its research, the most important predictors of a child developing an integrated faith were:

- the frequency of discussions about faith with their mother or father
- the frequency of family prayer (exclusive of meals), family devotions, and Bible study
- the frequency with which *parents and children together* were involved in activities to serve others
- lifetime involvement in church/exposure to Christian education (which finished *fourth*)[5]

These findings confirm what many of us already know—that the family plays a critical role in the spiritual development in children. What happens in the time kids spend with their parents is probably more important in their overall spiritual development than the experiences they have at church. For reasons I'll describe later in this chapter, family influence may be of even greater importance when kids are affected by mental illness or other types of disability.

To turn the ship around, an integrated approach to ministry characterized by leaders from all departments in the church working together with a common purpose will be required. *An inclusion ministry that addresses the needs of all family members has the greatest potential for impact.*

In the last chapter, I referred to Libby Peterson's work in promoting relationships between families in the church and families of kids with disabilities. Libby described the essentials of a discipleship approach most likely to produce the desired benefits in families impacted by mental illness:

> We have clarified the Biblical principles around parenting, marriage and faith training—these undergird all we do with parents. The principles emphasize things like: parents are called to be the primary faith trainers for their kids, the home is to be the center of faith formation and the church is here to help. We teach four "fantastic faith forming family functions"—Talk, Pray, Read, Serve—encouraging parents to talk with their kids about the Lord, pray together as a family, read the Bible together and serve together. We consistently teach that the most important thing that any parent can do for their kids is to tend to the vitality of their own personal relationship with the Lord. Additionally we try to consistently remind ourselves that ministry always travels along relational lines . . . Parents need discipleship—to fall in love again with Christ—and encouragement to share what they know and are consistently learning with their kids. The church is here to HELP. Too often churches talk about partnering with parents when the church is in fact taking the LEAD and expecting parents to get on board with their initiatives.[6]

HOW MINISTRY LEADERS CAN LEVERAGE THE INFLUENCE OF FAMILIES

Reggie Joiner is a prominent leader in the family ministry movement and the author of *Think Orange,* a book that articulates many of the principles that undergird the movement. In the book, he introduces the 3,000/40 principle, which is based on the observation that a typical kid spends three thousand hours per year with their parents and forty hours per year in church-related activities.[7] Our goal as the church is to implement a strategy to build faith and character in kids with mental illness, as well as in their siblings, who may or may not have mental illness. Reggie argues that church leaders are likely to have the greatest impact through leveraging the three thousand hours per year kids spend with their parents as opposed to pouring all our resources into the forty hours each year the kids spend at church.

Reggie's principle is especially relevant when families are raising kids with mental illness—or any other disability. Parents are likely to have more opportunities to interact with their kids compared to families where no disability is present, for all the reasons I've already described in the preceding chapters—stigma, anxiety, peer conflicts, and social isolation. Parents are also more likely to have a better sense of how to communicate most effectively with their child than will someone serving as a children's ministry staff person or volunteer.

The role of children's and student ministry leaders in a mental health inclusion ministry is to come alongside parents, extended family members, and other caregivers with resources and support. Ministry leaders provide help and encouragement to parents who are exercising their responsibilities to guide and cultivate spiritual growth in their children. Parents of kids with mental health issues may require more resources and support from their church than other families do. Some may feel completely inadequate for the task of directing their child's spiritual development because they themselves missed out on church when they were young. Some learn how to be disciples through shepherding their own children.

Here are three ways church leaders can support parents when kids have mental health concerns:

- They can help kids and parents prioritize what to study in the Bible while providing parents with the necessary resources to teach key biblical concepts and principles to their children.

- They can prompt kids and parents to practice spiritual disciplines. Kids with common mental health conditions greatly benefit from cultivating habits but struggle with the process of forming habits. Help them through encouragement and reminders.
- They can provide parents with the motivation and resources necessary for initiating spiritual conversations with their kids.

The need for support may be especially acute when parents are unable to care for their children because of their own mental illness or perhaps the substance abuse that results from attempting to self-medicate the symptoms of their mental illness. Grandparents and other extended family members often find themselves in the position of assuming the parents' responsibilities, including their responsibility for their children's spiritual growth.

IT TAKES A CHURCH TO RAISE A CHILD WITH MENTAL ILLNESS

Families impacted by mental illness need churches that are intentional about community. Rates of mental illness are substantially higher among single parents. Single female parents are twice as likely and single male parents nearly four times as likely to experience common mental disorders than married parents.[8] Higher divorce rates may result in less consistent church participation for kids. Parents may have more difficulty staying involved at church because of their own functional limitations.

Kids with mental illness—or kids of parents with mental illness—greatly benefit from relationships with other adults from outside of their families who take an interest in them and model the beliefs and character traits the parents are seeking to instill at home. Because of the social isolation described earlier in the book, they're less likely to have opportunities for those relationships outside of a church. If a parent becomes ill or is temporarily disabled, other adults in the church may need to provide child care, supervision, or support.

ADOPTION AND FOSTER CARE MINISTRIES

I'm convinced that the impetus for mental health inclusion initiatives in many churches will come from the needs of families who serve in adoption and foster care ministries. Pregnancy rates among teenage girls in Canada with major mental illness (psychotic disorders, bipolar disorder, major depression) are three times higher than in the general population.[9] Parental mental illness is a contributing factor to the neglect and abuse that can necessitate foster care placement.

I'm aware of many prominent theologically and socially conservative Christians who have experienced firsthand the challenges involved in raising adoptive and foster children with serious mental health issues. Their stories are helpful in enhancing awareness of the support needs of families serving in these ministries and changing old perceptions that mental illness in children is a result of insufficient faith or inadequate parenting.

Adopted children have a twofold to threefold greater risk of common mental health conditions and are roughly four times more likely to attempt suicide compared to the general population.[10] At the 2010 American Academy of Child and Adolescent Psychiatry Research Forum, Dr. Julie Zito presented data examining the use of psychiatric medication among children in the foster care system in Texas showing that kids in foster care were five times as likely as other kids covered under Medicaid to be taking psychiatric medication, and nearly three quarters of the foster children taking medicine were on at least two medications.[11]

Church leaders who encourage participation in adoption and foster care ministries have a responsibility to put in place the supports to allow the family to maintain no less than their preexisting level of engagement in the church. Is your church prepared to welcome their kids into your children's ministry or youth ministry? Will your church provide the parents with the support they need to continue attending their weekly small group? What about the support they need to continue serving in ministries where they've grown and matured in their faith? I believe it's unchristian for churches to promote adoption and foster care ministries without committing to support them at every point in their journey.

■   ■   ■

This chapter was intentionally placed at the end of the book, because it ties together so much of what we've come to understand regarding mental illness, families, and the church. A successful mental health inclusion initiative requires each ministry to work together for a common purpose. We must be prepared to welcome any member of the family so that every member of the family may experience Jesus through the ministries of the local church. This initiative represents a synergy between two God-ordained institutions—the church and the family. Ultimately, inclusion ministry is God's means of restoring the church to what it was meant to be:

> If one part suffers, every part suffers with it; if one part is honored, every part rejoices with it.
>
> Now you are the body of Christ, and each one of you is a part of it.
>
> *1 Corinthians 12:26–27*

I'm looking forward to hearing the stories of kids and families impacted through your ministry. Let's get started!

Taking the First Step—Together

A few days later, when Jesus again entered Capernaum, the people heard that he had come home. They gathered in such large numbers that there was no room left, not even outside the door, and he preached the word to them. Some men came, bringing to him a paralyzed man, carried by four of them. Since they could not get him to Jesus because of the crowd, they made an opening in the roof above Jesus by digging through it and then lowered the mat the man was lying on. When Jesus saw their faith, he said to the paralyzed man, "Son, your sins are forgiven."

MARK 2:1–5

This passage from Mark's Gospel is a fabulous illustration of what the church should be all about—and it encapsulates my purpose in writing this book. The families I've come to know through my practice are affected by conditions that make it hard for them to enter the buildings where they can experience the presence of Jesus.

What I love about this story is the faithfulness of the friends of the man who was paralyzed and their determination to get their friend in front of Jesus. The mat their friend is confined to represents deadweight. They need a plan for carrying him up what was likely a narrow ladder to lift him onto the roof. They need to obtain tools to cut through the roof, as well as ropes and pulleys to lower their friend safely into the room. They need to determine where Jesus is situated in the room and take care not to injure anyone from falling debris as they cut through the roof. They also needed to consider the time and expense involved with repairing the roof when they were finished.

There's so much truth packed into the first twelve verses of Mark 2. Jesus' first words were to tell the man experiencing paralysis that his sins were forgiven. He pointed out that this man, like each of us, has a much more serious condition (sin) and a much deeper need for forgiveness than for healing from any physical or mental disability we might experience in this life.

I'm most struck by this brief phrase in verse 5 (emphasis added): "when Jesus saw *their* faith." To what extent does God work in the lives of our friends and neighbors because of the collective efforts and faithfulness of his people organized through the church? The friends weren't seeking some benefit for themselves; rather, their collective faithfulness was directed at trying to get their friend in front of Jesus. This passage is a wonderful illustration of what church should be all about. The church exists not for ourselves, but to put our friends and neighbors in front of Jesus.

Who might Jesus bring to faith if the people in your church resolve to work together to remove whatever obstacles are getting in the way for many of your friends and neighbors who need to experience Jesus? What might Jesus do if each person in your church was willing to grab a corner of the mat as a way to support those in your community impacted by mental illness?

Are you willing to take the first step for your friends and neighbors who don't know Jesus?

Continuing our analogy from Mark 2, this book has given you a blueprint to the house where your friends and neighbors can find Jesus and tools for lifting them onto the roof of the house, cutting through the roof without making too much of a mess, and safely helping them enter Jesus' presence. What you and your church do with the blueprints and the tools is now up to you.

If you're a senior pastor or senior leader in your church, pray for discernment and direction. Pursue buy-in from your staff and your church's governing board or authority for implementing a mental health inclusion plan.

If you are a church staff member, volunteer or lay leader, approach your church's senior pastor (or senior leadership team) to obtain their support and guidance as to the most appropriate ways to move forward.

If your church's leadership responds by saying either no or not yet to your plans, consider how you might implement any of the ideas and strategies described in this book while remaining respectful and obedient to your church's leadership. The church is present wherever God's people are present and about the work of expanding God's kingdom. You are the church! Your ministry "win" occurs whenever any person with a mental health condition or any family member of someone with a mental health condition experiences Jesus through the people and ministry of a local church. If you're acting on a call to help someone with mental illness experience Jesus, your church is doing mental health inclusion ministry, regardless of whether your ministry receives official recognition by the church.

Borrowing again from Mark's illustration, no one carries the mat by themselves. In this book's introduction, I shared that the intent of our team at Key Ministry is to provide relationship and resources for churches pursuing disability ministry. I'd like to invite you to join an online community we've established on Facebook for mental health inclusion ministry leaders. Our online communities are "closed groups" that require a brief registration process. Registration can be accessed through our mental health resources page at www.keyministry.org.

Leaders of other Christian organizations involved with mental health ministry belong to our online community. We look forward to a mutual exchange of knowledge, experience, and resources as you grow your ministry.

Our team has been hard at work in producing mental health inclusion ministry training resources. As this book's final revisions were sent to the publisher, seven training videos to accompany this book have been filmed, with many more to come. I invite you to follow Key Ministry on Facebook and Twitter and to subscribe to our ministry's blog for church leaders at www.church4everychild.org for news of new training resources and opportunities.

We look forward to coming alongside as you take your next step in mental health inclusion ministry. If you have questions or concerns that haven't been addressed in the book, we're delighted to make ourselves available to you or your church's inclusion team. To contact us, go to www.keyministry.org/consulting and give us a brief description of your request. Someone from our team will follow up with you.

We'd be honored to come alongside you and your church to lend a hand with your mat—the mat holding your friends, neighbors, and loved ones touched by mental illness who need to experience Jesus.

Acknowledgments

As iron sharpens iron,
so one person sharpens another.

PROVERBS 27:17

God used many different people with different gifts and passions in building Key Ministry and imparting this blueprint for ministry with persons with mental illness and their families.

None of this work would have been possible had it not been for Libby Peterson's faithfulness in responding to the needs of families served by the children's ministry at Bay Presbyterian Church twenty years ago, or Hu Auburn's willingness as a senior pastor to leverage the time, talent, and treasure of his church's people to start an organization fifteen years ago that would help other churches minister to kids with "hidden disabilities." Key Ministry would not have been possible without a church willing to encourage and resource "entrepreneurs for Christ" with big ideas for sharing the gospel with others in need of the love of Christ.

God also saw fit to bless Key Ministry with a number of extremely gifted and passionate leaders who made our ministry and this work better before moving on to other ministry opportunities. I owe much of my understanding of disability ministry to Katie Wetherbee, an early Key Ministry volunteer and staff member who has done much to advance the cause of special needs ministry in the church. Harmony Hensley is another former staff member whose insight and experience in designing physical spaces and environments to support ministry is reflected throughout this work. Shannon Dingle enhanced our understanding of the mental health and trauma-related challenges involved in adoption and foster care ministries. Prior to and during his time serving as a member of our ministry team, Nils Smith contributed greatly to our knowledge of how social media alongside other new and emerging technologies can be used to advance mental health ministry.

Finally, I'm grateful to two members of our current ministry team, Sandra Peoples and Beth Golik, for their outstanding work in advancing the mission of Key Ministry during the time I've been preoccupied with bringing this work to completion.

While God saw fit to bring the right people with the right mix of gifts, talents, and passions to our Key Ministry team over the past fifteen years, he also connected us with the right people to bring this book project to fruition. I'm grateful that the well-known Christian author and trauma expert Jolene Philo introduced me to Karen Neumair from Credo Communications. Karen was able to open the right doors at HarperCollins/Zondervan and helped them recognize the need for this work. I'm also grateful for the contributions of Ryan Pazdur and Dirk Buursma, my editors at Zondervan, who asked lots of great questions and contributed many ideas that made this work more useful.

Notes

Chapter 1: The Disconnect

1. "Any Mental Illness (AMI) Among U.S. Adults: Prevalence of Any Mental Illness Among U.S. Adults (2015)," National Institute of Mental Health, www.nimh.nih.gov/health/statistics/prevalence/any -mental-illness-ami-among-us-adults.shtml (accessed July 6, 2017).
2. Sussana N. Visser et al., "Trends in the Parent-Report of Health Care Provider-Diagnosed and Medicated Attention-Deficit/Hyperactivity Disorder: United States, 2003–2011," *Journal of the American Academy of Child and Adolescent Psychiatry* 53.1 (January 2014): 34–46.e2, www.jaacap.com/article/S0890-8567(13)00594-7/fulltext (accessed July 6, 2017).
3. Kathleen Ries Merikangas et al., "Service Utilization for Lifetime Mental Health Disorders in U.S. Adolescents: Results from the National Comorbidity Survey—Adolescent Supplement (NCS-A)," *Journal of the American Academy of Child and Adolescent Psychiatry* 50.1 (January 2011): 32–45, www.ncbi.nlm.nih.gov/pmc/articles/ PMC4408275 (accessed July 6, 2017); see "Anxiety Disorders," National Alliance on Mental Illness, www.nami.org/Learn-More/ Mental-Health-Conditions/Anxiety-Disorders (accessed July 6, 2017).
4. "Statistics: Major Depression among Adults," National Institute of Mental Health (2015), www.nimh.nih.gov/health/statistics/prevalence/ major-depression-among-adults.shtml (accessed July 6, 2017).

5. "Statistics: Any Anxiety Disorder among Adults, National Institute of Mental Health (2015), www.nimh.nih.gov/health/statistics/prevalence/any-anxiety-disorder-among-adults.shtml (accessed July 6, 2017).

6. "Statistics: Suicide," National Institute of Mental Health (2015), www.nimh.nih.gov/health/statistics/suicide/index.shtml (accessed July 6, 2017).

7. "Study of Acute Mental Illness and Christian Faith: Research Report," LifeWay Research (2014), http://lifewayresearch.com/wp-content/uploads/2014/09/Acute-Mental-Illness-and-Christian-Faith-Research-Report-1.pdf (accessed July 6, 2017).

8. Matthew S. Stanford, "Demon or Disorder: A Survey of Attitudes toward Mental Illness in the Christian Church," *Mental Health, Religion and Culture* 10.5 (September 2007): 445–49, www.baylor.edu/content/services/document.php/35617.pdf (accessed July 6, 2017).

9. For more information, visit the Joni and Friends website at www.joniandfriends.org.

10. A common treatment strategy for patients suffering from obsessive-compulsive disorder is to provide distraction from recurrent, intrusive thoughts. Scripture suggests Saul was tormented by the realization he had been rejected by God as king and by the evidence that God's favor was upon David. David's music initially brought Saul relief by serving as a distraction from his obsessive thoughts. As Saul's obsessions became increasingly severe (see 1 Samuel 18:10–11), he twice attempted to kill David by hurling his spear at him. Extreme irritability and violent behavior are not uncommon in my experience of treating patients unable to obtain relief from their obsessive thinking.

11. Cited in Stephen Grcevich, "Including Kids and Teens with Mental Illness at Church ... What Are the Barriers?" Church4EveryChild, January 28, 2014, https://church4everychild.org/2014/01/28/including-kids-and-teens-with-mental-illness-at-church-what-are-the-barriers (accessed July 6, 2017).

Chapter 2: A Different Type of Disability

1. "U.S. Code, Title 42, Chapter 126, § 12102—Definition of Disability," *Cornell Law School: Legal Information Institute*, www.law.cornell.edu/uscode/text/42/12102 (accessed July 6, 2017).

2. "Mental Health Conditions," National Alliance on Mental Illness, www.nami.org/Learn-More/Mental-Health-Conditions (accessed July 6, 2017).

3. American Psychiatric Association, *Diagnostic and Statistical Manual of Mental Disorders*, 5th ed. (Arlington, VA: American Psychiatric Association Publishing, 2013), 20.

4. Cited in Stephen Grcevich, "Casseroles, Church, and the Stigma of Kids with Mental Illness," Church4EveryChild, January 29, 2014, https://church4everychild.org/2014/01/29/casseroles-church-and-the -stigma-of-kids-with-mental-illness (accessed July 6, 2017).

5. See Jay E. Adams, "What Is 'Nouthetic' Counseling?" Institute for Nouthetic Studies, www.nouthetic.org/about-ins/what-is-nouthetic -counseling (accessed July 6, 2017).

6. See Micah Russell, "The Education System: 'Now Climb That Tree,'" *The Marquette Educator*, July 12, 2012, https://marquetteeducator .wordpress.com/2012/07/12/climbthattree (accessed July 6, 2017).

7. See Susanna N. Visser et al., "Trends in the Parent-Report of Health Care Provider-Diagnosed and Medicated Attention-Deficit/ Hyperactivity Disorder: United States, 2003–2011," *Journal of the American Academy of Child and Adolescent Psychiatry* 53.1 (January 2014): 34–46.e2, www.jaacap.com/article/S0890-8567(13)00594-7/ fulltext (accessed July 6, 2017).

8. See James J. Hudziak and Stephen V. Faraone, "The New Genetics in Child Psychiatry," *Journal of the American Academy of Child and Adolescent Psychiatry* 49:8 (August 2010): 729–35, www.jaacap.com/ article/S0890-8567(10)00495-8/fulltext (accessed July 6, 2017).

9. See Ronald C. Kessler et al., "Prevalence, Severity, and Comorbidity of Twelve-Month *DSM-IV* Disorders in the National Comorbidity Survey Replication," *Archives of General Psychiatry* 62.6 (June 2005): 617–27, https://pdfs.semanticscholar.org/8775/ebd1e6564d41e87168 1d7daa21208df9fc21.pdf (accessed July 6, 2017).

10. Benjamin T. Conner, *Amplifying Our Witness: Giving Voice to Adolescents with Developmental Disabilities* (Grand Rapids: Eerdmans, 2012), 22.

Chapter 3: The First Two Barriers to Church Involvement

1. Ed Stetzer, "Mental Illness and the Church: New Research on Mental Health from LifeWay Research," *Christianity Today*, September 17, 2013, www.christianitytoday.com/edstetzer/2013/september/mental-illness-and-church-new-research-on-mental-health-fro.html (accessed July 6, 2017).

2. Stetzer, "Mental Illness and the Church."

3. Albert Ellis, "Rational Psychotherapy and Individual Psychology," *All About Psychology*, www.all-about-psychology.com/rational-psychotherapy.html (accessed July 6, 2017).

4. Jay E. Adams, *Competent to Counsel: Introduction to Nouthetic Counseling* (1970; repr., Grand Rapids: Zondervan, 1986).

5. Adams, *Competent to Counsel*, 29.

6. Adams, *Competent to Counsel*, 29, italics in the original.

7. Jay E. Adams, *The Christian Counselor's Manual: The Practice of Nouthetic Counseling* (1973; repr., Grand Rapids: Zondervan, 2010), 9.

8. Stephen Grcevich, "Sin, Mental Illness, and Disability Ministry," *Church4EveryChild*, June 19, 2014, https://drgrcevich.wordpress.com/2014/06/19/sin-mentalillness-disabilityministry (accessed July 6, 2017).

9. John MacArthur, "God's Pattern for Children, Part Two," *Grace to You*, March 31, 1996, www.gty.org/resources/sermons/1949/Gods-Pattern-for-Children-Part-2 (accessed July 6, 2017).

10. John Rosemond and Bose Ravenel, MD, *The Diseasing of America's Children: Exposing the ADHD Fiasco and Empowering Parents to Take Back Control* (Nashville: Nelson, 2008), 4–5.

Chapter 4: Five Additional Barriers

1. See William L. Hathaway and Russell A. Barkley, "Self-Regulation, ADHD, and Child Religiousness," *Journal of Psychology and Christianity* 22.2 (2003): 101–14, www.researchgate.net/publication/232557922_Self-regulation_ADHD_child_religiousness (accessed July 6, 2017). This paper offers an excellent description of executive functioning as it pertains to spiritual development in children and adults with ADHD.

2. See Russell A. Barkley, "Behavioral Inhibition, Sustained Attention, and Executive Functions: Constructing a Unifying Theory of ADHD," *Psychological Bulletin* 121.1 (January 1997): 65–94, https://pdfs.semantic scholar.org/78fc/ab288d57fb7f356404e72dfc9bbcf19f90fc.pdf (accessed July 6, 2017).

3. See Philip A. Fisher et al., "The Combined Effects of Prenatal Drug Exposure and Early Adversity on Neurobehavioral Disinhibition in Childhood and Adolescence," *Development and Psychopathology* 23.2 (August 2011): 777–88, https://pdfs.semanticscholar.org/a003/9e32f 274d2dc70d4b511600ad92f82714882.pdf (accessed July 6, 2017).

4. Cited in Roianne R. Ahn et al., "Prevalence of Parents' Perceptions of Sensory Processing Disorders among Kindergarten Children, *American Journal of Occupational Therapy* 58 (2004): 287–93, https://pdfs. semanticscholar.org/7578/eab52b53a96c1423e668f85fb21fb7020e17 .pdf?_ga=2.72330643.1002991078.1500814854-699433840.1500814854 (accessed July 6, 2017).

5. See Julia P. Owen et al., "Abnormal White Matter Microstructure in Children with Sensory Processing Disorders," *NeuroImage: Clinical* 2 (2013): 844–53, www.sciencedirect.com/science/article/pii/S2213158 213000776 (accessed July 6, 2017).

6. Beth Arky, "Sensory Processing Issues Explained," Child Mind Institute, https://childmind.org/article/sensory-processing-issues-explained (accessed July 6, 2107).

7. Rick Warren, *The Purpose Driven Life* (Grand Rapids: Zondervan, 2002).

8. Max Lucado, *Fearless: Imagine Your Life without Fear* (Nashville: Nelson, 2009), 144.

9. See Eddie Cole, "Belong, Believe, Become: A New Process of Evangelism," *Christianity Today*, February 14, 2017, www.christianitytoday.com/ edstetzer/2017/january/church-growth.html (accessed July 6, 2017).

10. See Carey Nieuwhof, "10 Things That Demonstrate The World You Grew Up In No Longer Exists," December 28, 2016, http://carey nieuwhof.com/10-things-that-demonstrate-the-world-you-grew-up-in -no-longer-exists (accessed July 6, 2017).

11. Cited in Deborah Fauntleroy, Christine Fluet, and Lisa Lambert, "Respite Care: What Families Say," Parent/Professional Advocacy

League and the Massachusetts Department of Mental Health (February 2013), http://ppal.net/wp-content/uploads/2011/01/Repite-Care-What-Families-Say.pdf (accessed July 6, 2017).

12. See Joe Sutton, "Understanding Mildly Disabled Students in Christian Schools," BJU Press, October 21, 2015), www.bjupress.com/resources/articles/t2t/understanding-mildly-disabled-students-in-christian-schools.php (accessed July 6, 2017).

13. See Tammy Bachrach, "Open the Door of Christian Education to *All* Students: A Call for Christian School Reform," *Justice, Spirituality and Education Journal* 3.1 (Spring 2015): 16–26, http://education.biola.edu/static/media/downloads/bachrach.pdf (accessed July 6, 2017).

14. See Deborah Dewey et al., "Developmental Coordination Disorder: Associated Problems in Attention, Learning, and Psychosocial Adjustment," *Human Movement Science* 21.5–6 (December 2002): 905–18, www.sciencedirect.com/science/article/pii/S016794570200163X (accessed July 6, 2017).

15. See Daniel Rasic et al., "Risk of Mental Illness in Offspring of Parents with Schizophrenia, Bipolar Disorder, and Major Depressive Disorder: A Meta-Analysis of Family High-Risk Studies," *Schizophrenia Bulletin* 40.1 (2014): 28–38, www.medscape.com/viewarticle/819416 (accessed July 6, 2017).

16. Nancy C. P. Low et al., "The Association between Parental History of Diagnosed Mood/Anxiety Disorders and Psychiatric Symptoms and Disorders in Young Adult Offspring," *BMC Psychiatry* 12 (2012): 188, https://bmcpsychiatry.biomedcentral.com/articles/10.1186/1471-244X-12-188 (accessed July 6, 2017).

Chapter 5: What Can Churches Do to Help?

1. Many of the fastest-growing evangelical churches most committed to community outreach employ a "simple church" model in which resources are devoted to the most essential church functions so that ministries in the church avoid competing with one another for time, attention, money, volunteers, and participation. See Thom S. Rainer and Eric Geiger, *Simple Church: Returning to God's Process for Making Disciples*, rev. ed. (Nashville: B&H, 2011).

2. See Edward B. Rogers, Matthew Stanford, and Diana R. Garland, "The Effects of Mental Illness on Families within Faith Communities," *Mental Health, Religion and Culture* 15.3 (2012): 301–13. www.tandfonline.com/doi/abs/10.1080/13674676.2011.573474 (accessed July 6, 2017).

3. Andy Stanley and Lane Jones, *Communicating for a Change* (Colorado Springs: Multnomah, 2006).

4. See Anna V. Fisher, Karrie E. Godwin, and Howard Seltman, "Visual Environment, Attention Allocation, and Learning in Young Children: When Too Much of a Good Thing May Be Bad," *Psychological Science* 25.7 (2014): 1362–70, http://citeseerx.ist.psu.edu/viewdoc/download;jsessionid=57C4D9A27FFCD7F68EE6C1962A55C7FE?doi=10.1.1.704.5598&rep=rep1&type=pdf (accessed July 6, 2017).

5. Cited in Stephen Grcevich, "Mental Health Inclusion: Creating More Welcoming Ministry Environments," Church4EveryChild, May 26, 2015, https://church4everychild.org/2015/05/28/mental-health-inclusion-creating-more-welcoming-ministry-environments (accessed July 6, 2017).

6. From the Key Ministry website at www.keyministry.org/mission-churches.

7. Greg L. Hawkins and Cally Parkinson, *Reveal: Where Are You?* (South Barrington, IL: Willow Creek Association, 2007).

8. See Ed Stetzer, "The Church and Mental Illness Part 1: Aspirations v. Reality," *Christianity Today*, December 2, 2014, www.christianitytoday.com/edstetzer/2014/october/church-and-mental-illness-part-1-aspirations-v-reality.html (accessed July 6, 2017); "Study of Acute Mental Illness and Christian Faith: Research Report," LifeWay Research (2014), http://lifewayresearch.com/wp-content/uploads/2014/09/Acute-Mental-Illness-and-Christian-Faith-Research-Report-1.pdf (accessed July 6, 2017).

9. Perry Noble, *Overwhelmed*: *Winning the War against Worry* (Downers Grove, IL: Tyndale, 2014).

10. Jessica Martinez, "Pastor Perry Noble Gets Candid about Struggle with Depression in New Book 'Overwhelmed,'" *Christian Post*, March 21, 2014, www.christianpost.com/news/pastor-perry-noble-gets-candid-about-struggle-with-depression-in-new-book-overwhelmed-interview-116548 (accessed July 6, 2017).

11. Amy Simpson, "10 Ways Mental Illness Is Stigmatized in the Church," June 17, 2013. http://amysimpsononline.com/2013/06/10-ways-mental -illness-is-stigmatized-in-the-church (accessed July 6, 2017).

12. "10 Leading Causes of Death by Age Group, United States—2015," National Center for Injury Prevention and Control, CDC, www .cdc.gov/injury/images/lc-charts/leading_causes_of_death_age _group_2015_1050w740h.gif (accessed July 6, 2017).

13. See "Prevalence: Any Anxiety Disorder Among Adults," National Insti- tute of Mental Health, www.nimh.nih.gov/health/statistics/prevalence/ any-anxiety-disorder-among-adults.shtml (accessed July 6, 2017); "Prevalence: Any Anxiety Disorder Among Children," National Institute of Mental Health www.nimh.nih.gov/health/statistics/prevalence/ any-anxiety-disorder-among-children.shtml (accessed July 6, 2017).

14. "What Is Khesed?" www.khesedwellness.com/about (accessed July 6, 2017).

15. "Homelessness and Housing," Substance Abuse and Mental Health Services Administration (June 2016), www.samhsa.gov/homelessness -housing (accessed July 6, 2017).

16. Doris J. James and Lauren E. Glaze, "Mental Health Problems of Prison and Jail Inmates," Bureau of Justice Statistics, December 14, 2006, www.bjs.gov/content/pub/pdf/mhppji.pdf (accessed July 6, 2017).

17. Visit them online at www.mentalhealthgracealliance.org (accessed July 6, 2017).

18. Joe Padilla, "5 Steps to the Rise of Mental Health Support in the Church," Church4EveryChild, June 3, 2015, https://church4every child.org/2015/06/03/joe-padilla-5-steps-to-the-rise-of-mental-health -support-in-the-church (accessed July 6, 2017).

19. For more information, visit National Alliance on Mental Illness, www .nami.org/Find-Support/NAMI-Programs/NAMI-Family-to-Family (accessed July 6, 2017).

20. For more information, visit National Alliance on Mental Illness, https://www.nami.org/Find-Support/NAMI-Programs/NAMI-Basics (accessed July 6, 2017).

21. For more information, visit National Alliance on Mental Illness, https:// www.nami.org/Extranet/Education-Training-and-Outreach-Programs/ Outreach-and-Advocacy/NAMI-FaithNet (accessed July 6, 2017).

22. For more information, visit Fresh Hope, http://freshhope.us/about
-fresh-hope (accessed July 6, 2017).

23. For more information, visit the Grace Alliance, http://mentalhealth
gracealliance.org/family-grace-groups (accessed July 6, 2017).

24. Edward B. Rogers and Matthew S. Stanford, "A Church-Based Peer-
Led Group Intervention for Mental Illness," *Mental Health, Religion
and Culture* 18:6 (2015): 470–81, http://www.tandfonline.com/doi/
full/10.1080/13674676.2015.1077560 (accessed July 6, 2017).

25. Libby Peterson, "Belong to Believe," Church4EveryChild, September
29, 2013, https://church4everychild.org/2013/09/29/belong-to-believe
-libby-peterson (accessed July 6, 2017).

26. "The Total Audience Report: Q1 2016," Nielsen Company, June 27,
2016, www.nielsen.com/us/en/insights/reports/2016/the-total-audience
-report-q1-2016.html (accessed July 6, 2017).

27. Luke Monahan and Caroline Renehan, *The Chaplain: A Faith Presence
in the School Community* (Dublin: Columba, 1998), 10.

28. Mary Glenn, "Ministry of Presence: Being a Safe for Teens," Fuller
Youth Institute, April 21, 2014, https://fulleryouthinstitute.org/
articles/ministry-of-presence (accessed July 6, 2007).

Chapter 6: Overcoming Stigma in the Church

1. Pastor Rick Warren, Facebook Live, May 19, 2017, www.facebook
.com/pastorrickwarren/videos/10155184051895903/?hc_ref=PAGES
_TIMELINE (accessed July 6, 2017).

2. "Study of Acute Mental Illness and Christian Faith: Research Report,"
LifeWay Research (2014), http://lifewayresearch.com/wp-content/
uploads/2014/09/Acute-Mental-Illness-and-Christian-Faith-Research
-Report-1.pdf (accessed July 6, 2017).

3. "Education and Resources," Mental Health Grace Alliance, http://mental
healthgracealliance.org/christian-mental-health-and-mental-illness/the
-answer-for-mental-illness-in-the-church22015 (accessed July 6, 2017).

Chapter 7: Overcoming Anxiety

1. David Zimmerman, "A Visitor's Perspective: An Embarrassing
Problem," Church Marketing Sucks, September 13, 2007, www.church

marketingsucks.com/2007/09/a-visitors-perspective-an-embarrassing-problem (accessed July 6, 2017).

2. Ted Cunningham, "Is Your Church Unnecessarily Uncomfortable?" Focus on the Family, November 9, 2015, http://blog.thrivingpastor.com/is-your-church-unnecessarily-uncomfortable (accessed July 6, 2017).

3. See Stephen Grcevich, "A Different Way of Looking at Mental Health Ministry," Key Ministry, November 20, 2016, www.keyministry.org/church4everychild/2016/11/20/a-different-way-of-looking-at-mental-health-ministry (accessed July 6, 2017).

4. Rhett Smith, *The Anxious Christian: Can God Use Your Anxiety for Good?* (Chicago: Moody, 2012).

5. Stephen Grcevich, "The Anxious Christian: Can God Use Your Anxiety for Good?" Key Ministry, July 26, 2016, www.keyministry.org/church4everychild/2016/7/26/the-anxious-christian-can-god-use-your-anxiety-for-good (accessed July 6, 2017).

Chapter 8: Overcoming Executive Functioning Weaknesses

1. John Piper, "Why Require Unregenerate Children to Act Like They're Good?" Desiring God, December 10, 2009, www.desiringgod.org/articles/why-require-unregenerate-children-to-act-like-they-re-good (accessed July 6, 2017).

2. See Kevin Rounding, Albert Lee, and Jill A. Jacobson, "Religion Replenishes Self-Control," *Psychological Science* 23.6 (May 2012): 635–42, http://journals.sagepub.com/doi/abs/10.1177/0956797611431987 (accessed July 6, 2017).

3. See Andy Stanley and Lane Jones, *Communicating for a Change* (Colorado Springs: Multnomah, 2006), 101–18.

4. Reggie Joiner, *Think Orange: Imagine the Impact When Church and Family Collide...* (Colorado Springs: Cook, 2009), 139.

5. Joiner, *Think Orange*, 138.

6. "Empowered To Connect Parent Training," Empowered To Connect, http://empoweredtoconnect.org/training (accessed July 6, 2017).

Chapter 9: Overcoming Sensory Processing Differences

1. See, for example, Harmony Hensley, "Welcoming Ministry Environments for Kids with ADHD, Part One," Church4EveryChild,

October 20, 2011, https://church4everychild.org/2010/10/20/harmony
-hensley-welcoming-ministry-environments-for-kids-with-adhd-part-one
(accessed July 6, 2017).

2. See Richard S. Colman et al., "The Effects of Fluorescent and Incandescent
Illumination upon Repetitive Behaviors in Autistic Children," *Journal of
Autism and Childhood Schizophrenia* 6.2 (June 1976): 157–62.

3. "SMPTE Standards Update: Cinema Audio Standards (2013)," Society
of Motion Pictures and Television Engineers, www.smpte.org/sites/
default/files/2013-03-12-Standards-Cinema_Audio-Vessa-v2.pdf
(accessed July 6, 2017).

4. "Occupational Safety and Health Standards: Occupational Noise
Exposure," Occupational Safety and Health Administration (December
2008), www.osha.gov/pls/oshaweb/owadisp.show_document?p_table
=standards&p_id=9735 (accessed July 6, 2017).

5. Emily Colson, "Darkness in a Theater," *Not Alone*, January 3, 2014,
http://specialneedsparenting.net/darkness-theater (accessed July 6, 2017).

6. Emily Colson, "Love to the Max," *Not Alone*, April 4, 2014, http://
specialneedsparenting.net/love-max (accessed July 6, 2017).

Chapter 10: Overcoming Social Communication Challenges

1. See Frank Newport, "Just Why Do Americans Attend Church?"
Gallup, April 6, 2007, www.gallup.com/poll/27124/just-why
-americans-attend-church.aspx#1 (accessed July 6, 2017).

2. See Thom S. Rainer, *Surprising Insights from the Unchurched and
Proven Ways to Reach Them* (Grand Rapids: Zondervan, 2008).

3. Ed Stetzer, "Community Matters: The Role of Transformational
Groups in the Church," *Christianity Today*, September 9, 2015, www
.christianitytoday.com/edstetzer/2015/september/community-matters
-role-of-transformational-groups-in-church.html (accessed July 6, 2017).

4. Mike Woods, "Church: The Friendliest Place in Town?" Church4Every
Child, September 14, 2014, https://church4everychild.org/2014/09/14/
church-the-friendliest-place-in-town-mike-woods (accessed July 6, 2017).

5. Katie Wetherbee and Rebecca Hamilton, "Sticks and Stones, Clicks
and Phones: Solutions for Preventing Bullying at Church," Key

Ministry, November 2012, https://vimeo.com/161405408 (accessed July 6, 2017).

6. See Chris Armstrong and Steven Gertz, "Got Your 'Spiritual Director' Yet?" *Christianity Today*, April 1, 2003, www.christianitytoday.com/ct/2003/aprilweb-only/4-28-51.0.html (accessed July 6, 2017).

Chapter 11: Overcoming Social Isolation

1. Libby Peterson, "The Church Has Left the Building," Church4EveryChild, November 5, 2012, https://church4everychild .org/2012/11/05/libby-peterson-the-church-has-left-the-building (accessed July 6, 2017).

Chapter 12: Overcoming Past Church Experience

1. See John W. Kennedy, "The 4-14 Window," *Christianity Today*, July 1, 2004, www.christianitytoday.com/ct/2004/july/37.53.html (accessed July 6, 2017).

2. See George Barna: *Transforming Kids into Spiritual Champions: Why Children Should Be Your #1 Priority* (2003; repr., Grand Rapids: Baker, 2014), 33–36.

3. Daniel Rasic et al., "Risk of Mental Illness in Offspring of Parents with Schizophrenia, Bipolar Disorder, and Major Depressive Disorder: A Meta-Analysis of Family High-Risk Studies," *Schizophrenia Bulletin* 40.1 (January 2014): 28–38, www.ncbi.nlm.nih.gov/pmc/articles/ PMC3885302 (accessed July 6, 2017).

4. Marina A. Bornovalova et al., "Familial Transmission and Heritability of Childhood Disruptive Disorders," *American Journal of Psychiatry* 167.9 (September 2010): 1066–74, www.ncbi.nlm.nih.gov/pmc/ articles/PMC2936682 (accessed July 6, 2017).

5. Peter L. Benson, Dorothy Williams, and Carolyn Eklin, *Effective Christian Education: A National Study of Protestant Congregations* (Minneapolis: Search Institute, 1990), www.searchinstitutepress.org/ faith_community_downloads/six_denominations.pdf (accessed July 6, 2017).

6. Libby Peterson, "'Thinking Orange': Libby Peterson on Partnering with Parents," Church4EveryChild, March 3, 2011, https://church4

everychild.org/2011/03/03/thinking-orange-libby-peterson-on
-partnering-with-parents (accessed July 6, 2017).

7. See Reggie Joiner, *Think Orange: Imagine the Impact When Church and Family Collide* . . . (Colorado Springs: Cook, 2009), 85.

8. See C. Cooper et al., "Depression and Common Mental Disorders in Lone Parents: Results of the 2000 National Psychiatric Morbidity Survey," *Psychological Medicine* 38.3 (March 2008): 335–42.

9. See Simone Vigod et al., "Fertility Rate Trends among Adolescent Girls with Major Mental Illness: A Population-Based Study," *Pediatrics* 133.3 (February 2014): e585–91, http://pediatrics.aappublications.org/content/early/2014/02/04/peds.2013-1761 (accessed July 6, 2017).

10. See Shannon Dingle, "What Are the Stats on Adoption, Trauma and Disability?" Church4EveryChild, February 16, 2016, https://church4everychild.org/2016/02/16/what-are-the-stats-on-adoption-trauma-and-disability (accessed July 6, 2017). This post provides an excellent overview (with links) to the most pertinent research describing rates of mental illness among adopted children and children in foster care.

11. See Stephen Grcevich, "Tales from the Research Front," Church4EveryChild, October 31, 2010), https://church4everychild.org/2010/10/31/tales-from-the-research-front (accessed July 6, 2017); see also Julie M. Zito et al., "Psychotropic Medication Patterns among Youth in Foster Care," *Pediatrics* 121.1 (January 2008): e157–63.